# PORTLAND FOOD CART STORIES

*Behind the Scenes with the*
*City's Culinary Entrepreneurs*

• • • • • • • • • • • • • • • • • • • • • • • • • • • • •

*Steven Shomler*

AMERICAN PALATE

Published by American Palate
A Division of The History Press
Charleston, SC 29403
www.historypress.net

Copyright © 2014 by Steven Shomler
All rights reserved

All photos by author unless otherwise noted.

First published 2014

Manufactured in the United States

ISBN 978.1.62619.373.4

Library of Congress CIP data applied for.

*This book is dedicated to all the chefs out there who are bootstrapping their way to a better life.*

# CONTENTS

# FOREWORD

December in Portland is a little different than December in my hometown of Austin. The wet Pacific Northwest weather didn't stave off my hunger for learning about the food carts, but the daily drizzle and gray chilled my Texas-thin blood to the bone.

While there on my initial trip, I slogged on some borrowed galoshes and rain gear and went to as many food carts as a girl could handle in a week. The amount of not just food carts but *really good* food carts is overwhelming, with several hundred being open each day. I found that Portland, like Austin, is a city that is passionate about supporting the local economy. As an outsider, I networked with Steven Shomler, Brett Burmeister, Scott Batchelar and all the local authorities to connect me to some of their favorite carts. After eating at almost fifty carts, "You should really come back in the spring," is what many who pitied my shivering would say. So, I booked another trip for April of the following year to enjoy Eat Mobile and fairer weather.

By then, I was working on the second volume of the Portland edition of the *Trailer Food Diaries Cookbook* series. I had eaten at tons of downtown carts and a few pods in little pockets peppered through the outskirts of main hubs. I conquered Eat Mobile, hugging some of my food cart friends from the previous years and eager to meet more new cart owners. After the festivities ended, it was Steven who really took me under his wing and said, "All right chick, I see that you want to do this and you want to do it right, so let me help you out." He planned my cart itinerary over the week I was there, personally taking me to cart openings and some of his favorite places, as well as some I had high on my wish list. The cart owners were consistently thrilled to see Steven, and he would immediately start photographing and tagging everyone on social media to document and promote the occasion.

After interviewing food cart/truck owners and collecting their recipes in more than ten states, I feel confident in saying that Portland is the true mecca of food carts because of their longevity, diversity and commitment to uniqueness in the market. And after spending time there with Steven, his passion is clear to me: he loves promoting food cart owners in order to share their stories and encourage their successes.

This book illustrates a portion of people in Portland willing to take their chance at living the American dream. Every walk of life is represented among the food cart owners, and their behind-the-scenes stories are fascinating. In his interviews, Steven found that most cart owners were working for six to seven days a week while they were starting up. They were willing to work eighty-plus hours a week to avoid working forty hours a week, all in pursuit of their own happiness and finding their own version of the American dream. Steven's first book is a tribute to all Portland's cart owners, acknowledging all it takes to be a bootstrap chef.

TIFFANY HARELIK
Author of the *Trailer Food Diaries Cookbook* series

# ACKNOWLEDGEMENTS

I am very grateful to the people who helped make this book possible.

Adam Whalen, thank you for insisting that I go with you that beautiful fall day in September 2010 to eat lunch at a food cart for the very first time in my life. My life is very different because of that day, and I am very grateful.

Al Gallo, thank you for all the inspiration and encouragement you have given me for the past twenty-five years or more.

Ken Wilson, thank you for being a terrific food cart wingman and for designing the Portland Food Cart Adventures logo, business cards and so on.

Kevin Brusett, thank you for providing me with life-changing, brand-legitimizing T-shirts.

Tiffany Harelik, thank for being kind enough to sit with me outside a food cart at a picnic table and listen to me tell you about the hopes I had to write a food cart book. Your "You can write that book, and I am happy to help you any way I can" comment meant more to me than you will ever know.

Many thanks to Molly Woodstock and Ken Wilson for helping out with taking some of photos found in this book. My deadline was looming, and you both came through.

Thank you to Pro Photo Supply and your awesome man behind the counter, Kevin, for helping me learn to take real photos with a real camera.

Lori Nold, thank you for all the care and kindness you provided my family and I over the summer, fall and winter of 2013. I don't think that I could have done this book without you.

Thank you to the people in my Dream Stoker Nation community and to all of my Facebook friends! The support you gave me as I worked on this book night after night was invaluable.

Thank you to my History Press commissioning editors Aubrie Koenig and Will McKay, as well as my production editor Ryan Finn. You were all awesome and incredibly helpful.

Thank you to the guys at CityTeam for putting up with my many absences at the end of 2013 as I finished up this book.

Thank you to Zayne Shomler for spending many Saturdays with me in the fall of 2013 as I took hundreds and hundreds of food cart photos. You were a big help, and I enjoyed spending those days with you so much.

Thank you to Zac, Zayne and Zoe Shomler for your ongoing encouragement and being understanding all those times that dad was monopolizing the computer so he could write.

Thank you to the bootstrap chefs featured in this book for trusting me with your precious stories. Much love to each of you.

Lastly and most importantly, thank you to my lovely wife, Gayla, for always believing in this book and in my dream to be an author and a speaker.

# INTRODUCTION

## WHAT'S IN THIS BOOK?

Within the pages of this book, you will find lots of stories—forty of them grouped into eight different parts.

There are stories of the owners of thirty different food carts. When I visit a food cart, I am always curious to know certain things: How did these people end up here doing this? Where did that name come from? Why this cuisine? And so on. The stories in here will provide answers to some of those questions.

I could have easily filled this book with in-depth stories of just five food cart owners; however, I wanted to give you, the reader, a sense of the incredible diversity that we have in Portland among our food cart owners. I chose to go the route of painting with a broad brush so you could get to know a number of my heroes.

Please note that I was not able to include every story I wanted to. For example, Nong's Khao Man Gai is a food cart that I really wanted to include but was not able to. Hopefully, I will be able to include the story of Nong and her great food cart in *Portland Food Cart Stories Vol. 2*.

## "What's Next," "When You Go" and "Recipes"

At the end of most of the food cart owners' stories, I have included additional postscripts. Every food cart owner I have met has big dreams, and the "What's Next" postscript gives you a window into a few of that particular food cart owner's hopes and dreams.

The "When You Go" postscript tells you what I would suggest that you eat when you visit that food cart.

Finally, I am a big fan of Tiffany Harelik. She is the author of the *Trailer Food Dairies Cookbook* series. To date, Tiffany has written two volumes featuring recipes from food carts right here in Portland. The "Recipes" postscript lets you know if that food cart has recipes in one of those volumes and occasionally other books as well.

## The Eight Parts of This Book

We start with an introduction to the Portland food cart scene. This section gives you an insider's view into this eclectic and entrepreneurial community. You are in this section right now.

Next we have the "Iconic Food Carts" section. These are some of the most popular and successful food carts here in Portland. These food carts are so well known that tourists visiting Portland seek them out, and their food is good enough to keep us locals coming back time and time again.

The second part tells you about eight people who heard the siren call and moved to Portland for the express purpose of opening a food cart. It is one thing to already live in Portland and roll the dice on a food cart venture. It is quite another to be daring enough to move across the country or the globe and take that risk.

Next comes breakfast! Portland has a well-deserved reputation as a great breakfast town. The "Breakfast!" part of this book will tell you about four carts that specialize in the first meal of the day.

The fourth part tells the stories of people and companies that do not own foods carts yet still are an important part of the Portland food cart scene.

The fifth part concerns vegetarian food carts. Of course Portland has vegetarian food carts. One of these four carts is actually vegan, and it is run by someone who wears tie-dyed T-shirts and loves the Grateful Dead.

The sixth part describes food carts that bring us delectable cuisine from around the world. In Portland, you can enjoy authentic food from places like the countries of Georgia, Norway and India; the island of Guam; the Mediterranean; and Asia.

Our final section is all about comfort food. I don't know about you, but sometimes I eat for comfort, and it does not get better than the food in this section—everything from mac and cheese to hamburgers and gumbo. Closing us out are boozy desserts from the Sugar B's, Liège-style waffles and some of the best coffee that you will ever have.

Interspersed between these eight parts are contributions from other food writers who love food carts as much as I do.

## *Go On Your Own Food Cart Adventure*

I hope that this book inspires you to get off the couch and head out on your own food cart adventure! If you happen to visit one the great food carts featured here in the volume, look for the *Portland Food Cart Stories* sticker and be sure to tell them that Steven sent you! Now, though, it's time for you to learn the facts about food carts.

# WHAT A FOOD CART REALLY IS

A question that is often asked is, "What is a food cart?" I have heard many stories of food cart owners trying to explain to friends and family who live in other parts of the country what it is they have started. Sometimes people envision a small pushcart. Basically, food carts are like food trucks.

## *Food Cart vs. Food Truck*

A food cart in Portland is like a food truck in any other part of the country with one *big* exception. Most of our food carts stay in one place; they don't drive from location to location. In fact, many Portland food carts aren't mobile at all.

Some Portland food carts are actual trucks, with engines and everything; some food carts are modified travel trailers; and other food carts have been built onto flatbed trailers from the floor up. Regardless of what the actual contraption is, in Portland we call them "food carts" rather than "food trucks" and "food trailers." If you want to eat at a food trailer, you'll have to go to Austin, Texas.

Part of the appeal of the Portland food cart scene is that you know where you need to go to find your favorite food cart. It's almost always there. All you need to worry about is whether or not it will be open when you want it to be. And that leads us to food cart pods.

## Food Cart Pods

Another very appealing part of the Portland food cart scene is our food cart pods. A food cart pod is a collection of food carts that are in one place. In Portland, we have two kinds of food cart pods, the first being the downtown pods that provide you with many food cart options in one area. When you buy from a downtown Portland food cart, you generally eat standing up or you take your meal back to your office.

The second type of food cart pod that we have is a neighborhood pod. The neighborhood pods have anywhere from two to about twenty food carts in one place. Many of these neighborhood pods offer covered seating, and some even have heated seating. A handful of the neighborhood pods have places where you can enjoy a beer with your meal, either from a beer garden built into the pod or from a pub that is adjoining the pod.

If you are visiting Portland and you want to see the Portland food cart scene, you really need to visit both a downtown pod and a neighborhood pod. Simply seeing one or the other is getting an incomplete picture.

At the end of 2013, Portland had more than thirty food cart pods and more than three hundred food carts.

## Food Carts Are Startups and Small Businesses

Most people don't realize that each and every food cart is a small business and, in the beginning, a startup. When you eat at a food cart, you are supporting small business and helping someone with his or her startup. Food cart owners who open a food cart face all the challenges that everyone else that launches a startup faces, and honestly, people with the kind of courage needed to start a business inspire me.

## *Bootstrap Chefs: The Best of the American Dream*

As noted chef and restaurateur Michael Symon said, "You do not have to go to school to be a chef...the title is earned by running a professional kitchen...although culinary school will help you reach your goals...and may speed up the process...it does not make you a chef."

People who start food carts do so because they have had a dream to be self-employed smoldering in their hearts and they are finally going for it. Many food cart owners have longed wished to be able to open their restaurant but lacked the $250,000 to $500,000 often required to do so. A food cart gives them a path to begin making that dream come true.

To me, food cart owners represent the best of the American dream; they are chefs who are bootstrapping their way to a better life. You want to know what a food cart really is? It is someone's hopes and dreams, and that is what this book is about: chefs who had the courage to battle for their dreams.

# MY FOOD CART STORY

On Friday, September 9, 2010, my friend Adam Whalen insisted that I join him at a food cart for lunch. My family and I had moved to Portland in the fall of 2004, and in the six years after that, I had never been to a food cart. In fact, the thought had never even crossed my mind.

That fateful September day, Adam took me to the Portland Soup Company Food Cart, and I had the mozzarella sandwich. This sandwich came with cart-made mozzarella, fresh basil, marinated Roma tomatoes, balsamic syrup and a roasted garlic aioli. I also bought the chilled tomato gazpacho with sweet corn and cilantro.

I was blown away by the food. It was so good, and I could not believe that something this good came out of kitchen in a little box. The next week, Adam took me to the Lardo Food Cart, and once again I could not believe how good the food was.

I had been toying with the idea of becoming a writer, and I told Adam that he and I should start a website and let everyone know how incredible

Portland food carts are. I told him that there had to be a number of idiots like me who have lived in Portland for years and completely overlooked these local treasures.

Time passed, and days turned in weeks. A year later, in the summer of 2011, I decided that I was going to become a speaker and an author and that I was going to start writing to make it happen. I was no longer going to play around with my writing. I was going to take it seriously and make a career of it. By that point in my journey, I had written enough to know the topics that I was going to write about, and food carts were going to be one of those topics.

In the fall of 2011, I started eating at many food carts. I told my wife that I was doing research for a website that I was going to launch. She smiled and wondered where this would all lead. On January 1, 2012, I launched the Portland Food Cart Adventures website, and I began writing about food carts.

## Food Cart Magic

The more I wrote about food carts and the more that I ate at them, the more impressed I became. To me, making such incredible food in a little box was nothing short of amazing, and I began to call this feat "food cart magic."

## How Can I Help These Entrepreneurs

I also got to know food cart owners, and I began to fall in love with them. I got to know their stories and hopes and dreams, as well as the huge obstacles they faced. I wanted to do what I could to help them make it. I began regularly consulting with food cart owners, helping them with things like having a successful startup, branding, marketing, social media and extending their brand.

I did not charge food cart owners for this advice. I wanted to serve them and help them. Even today, if you are a food cart owner or if you are going to be opening a food cart, if you buy me a cup of coffee (or a beer, or a whiskey), I will give you an hour or more of my time and my best advice.

I began to dream about having a festival in the summer here in Portland where food cart owners could make a killing and keep the proceeds of whatever they sold. In March 2012, I bought the domains PortlandFoodCartFestival.com and SummerFoodCartFestival.com.

The more I have served, the more good things have come my way. I remember the first time I got a call asking if I was willing to be filmed for show that would appear on the Food Network. My food cart website was less than six months old, and I was sure that I was being pranked.

To date, I have been privileged to be filmed for various food-related TV shows nine different times. My son Zayne will occasionally get texts from his friends that contain a picture of me on the paused TV, with the question, "Isn't that your dad?" One of my TV-related goals is to someday be a judge on *Iron Chef*.

## *The Portland Summer Food Cart Festival*

In the fall of 2012, I was contacted by a wonderful nonprofit that serves adults with disabilities, Adult Learning Systems of Oregon Inc., or ALSO. It had done a food cart event that past summer and wondered if I would help it plan an event featuring food carts for the next summer. I knew exactly what kind of event I wanted to see come together, and I knew exactly where I wanted this event to occur. I had been dreaming about this event since March, and I was very excited to help!

On June 22, 2013, the first annual Portland Summer Food Cart Festival took place at Mt. Hood Community College.

We had more than sixteen food carts, and more than 3,200 people showed up. We sold tickets for admission, and the ticket proceeds went to ALSO. The food carts that were part of this event got to sell their food, and they kept every dime they sold that day. Every single food cart owner who took part in the festival reported that June 22, 2013, was his or her best day for food sales ever. I was exhausted that evening when I went to bed; however, my heart was full.

## *I Am a Food Cart Fan*

I love being a part of the food cart community, and I am thrilled that the opportunity to write this book came along. I hope that you enjoy reading it as much as I enjoyed writing it.

*What's Next*: I am going to continue to write about food carts for my website, Portland Food Cart Adventures. I plan to continue to assist with the Portland Summer Food Cart Festival. I will continue to consult with food cart owners and do what I can to help them succeed. I am also going to expand my food writing beyond food carts. In 2014, I will be writing for GreatFoodGreatStories.com. Lastly, I hope that this book will sell well enough to allow me to write a *Portland Food Cart Stories*, vol. 2!

# PART I

# ICONIC FOOD CARTS

## A LIFE-CHANGING PLANE RIDE TO LA: KOi FUSION

Bo Kwon is the founder of what I call the KOi Fusion food cart empire. KOi Fusion has legions of fans, and Bo is arguably the most successful food cart owner in Portland. I sat down with Bo to interview him for this book, and my first question was, "When did you first think about starting a food cart?" This is his answer:

> *I was sitting on the couch talking to my dad about what to do because I knew that I was going to lose my job. The TV was on, and a news report came on about food trucks in LA becoming popular. I asked my dad if he would ever open a restaurant because I knew that he could cook. My dad said, "Why don't you open a food cart?" I started laughing. "A Korean food cart? Yeah right!" I few weeks later, I was sitting on the same couch, and I saw a Korean TV show talking about a new trend—the Korean taco.*

With that, things started to click with Bo, and he began to think about the possibility of opening a food cart that specialized in Korean tacos.

## Inspired by Roy Choi

Bo then heard about Roy Choi in LA, who was with the Korean taco food truck fleet known as Kogi. Bo began to hound and pester Roy, first with e-mails and then with phone calls. The response Bo consistently got was that Roy was busy.

Bo was convinced that somehow this guy in LA whom he had never met could help him with his dream of opening a food cart in Portland. Bo then did what any not-so-sane person with a dream would do: he called in sick one Monday, went to the airport, bought a plane ticket to LA and headed off to check out the food truck scene and hopefully find Roy.

By this point, Roy had opened a restaurant. Bo went to the restaurant and right into the kitchen, and there was Roy. Bo went over and tapped him on his shoulder. Bo said, "Hey, I just came from Portland." Roy said with astonishment, "You are that guy who has been bugging me about opening a food truck!"

Luckily, Roy said that he would give Bo five minutes. Bo's passion and commitment to his dream won Roy over. In those five minutes, Roy gave Bo hope and told him that he already had within himself all he needed to make a Korean food truck work in Portland.

Roy was doing what Bo wanted to do. Even though Bo had not met Roy until that day, Roy Choi had become an inspiration and hero to him. What meant the most to Bo was that Roy told him, "Go do Korean tacos in Portland. You have my blessing."

On the plane ride home, Bo felt like he had a new lease on life, and he now had the momentum, motivation and strength to start his business because of the blessing his hero had given him. A friendship was started, and along the way, Roy would occasionally give Bo feedback and counsel as KOi Fusion was getting launched.

## No Money and It Is Time to Buy a Cart

Following his meeting with Roy, Bo arrived back in Portland. A week later, all he had was his dream and the encouragement he received from Roy. He had no money and no credit, and now he needed to get a food cart so he could get started.

Bo found a taco truck in Hillsboro on the side of the road, and he went up to talk with the owner about buying it. Remember, Bo had no money. He bought a few tacos and then he asked the owner, "Would you want to sell me your food cart?" She laughed and said, "Very funny." Bo replied, "No, I'm serious. I really want to buy your food cart."

As it happened, the "owner" who was running this food cart had bought it for her son, who decided after opening the business that he did not really want to own a food cart. She was working the food cart to make the payments.

Bo proposed that he would buy the cart and they would hold the note. He would make monthly payments until he had paid the agreed-on amount in full. Bo also proposed that Rosie (the owner) stay on for the next six months, working in the cart and teaching Bo everything she knew. Bo did not know the first thing about running a food cart, and he realized that he needed to be schooled.

To entice Rosie to say yes to this whole arrangement, Bo said that he would hire Rosie and pay her an hourly wage and that he would make her monthly food truck payments. In addition, any profit the truck made in those six months would also go to her.

Bo said that those six months of learning to work in a taco truck selling Mexican food alongside Rosie was priceless. He learned a tremendous amount. He learned everything from dealing with gray water to insurance, hiring people and making handmade tortillas and pico de gallo. That experience working in a taco truck selling Mexican food is why the *fusion* in KOi Fusion is legitimate.

## The Name

The *KOi* in KOi Fusion is an acronym. It has nothing to do with koi fish or Japanese culture. KOi stands for "Korean Oregon infusion." Bo was born and raised right here in Oregon, and he is of Korean descent. He loves both Oregon and his Korean heritage, and he considers himself to be a fusion of both.

## Extending the Brand

The reason Bo made the leap from one food cart to two food carts was because while his first food cart was doing well, he realized that he still had no money to speak of and that if he was going to get where he wanted to

The KOi Fusion Food Cart at Mississippi Marketplace.

Bulgolgi BBQ Beef Taco with kimchi from KOi Fusion.

go, he was going to have to extend his food cart brand. That second food cart was actually a mobile truck, and it allowed him to start doing events and catering.

## *Kimchi*

One of my favorite Bo Kwon anecdotes is that when he was attending the University of Oregon, his roommates would not let him keep kimchi in the refrigerator. Now those same people love kimchi and are huge fans of Korean cuisine. The same thing can be said for the thousands of K headz (how KOi Fusion fans refer to themselves; the phrase is a riff on "sneakerheads," people who are rabid fans about sneakers, such as Bo) out there. All because Bo was willing to get on a plane and go to LA to pursue his dream.

*What's Next*: Bo plans on opening his first restaurant in the first half of 2014 on Division and then, late in 2014, he plans on opening a second restaurant on Burnside, near the Timbers stadium. Yes, those are ambitious goals. However, when I look at his track record, I know that Bo can accomplish whatever he sets his mind to.

*When You Go*: So many good things! I especially love the Bulgogi beef tacos and the Korean cheesesteak.

# OPEN 'TIL 3:00 A.M.: POTATO CHAMPION

When Mike McKinnon opened the Potato Champion Food Cart in April 2008 at the corner of 12th and Hawthorne, he changed Portland.

## *"I Had No Money and I Wanted to Quit My Job"*

Mike did not set out to change Portland. He simply wanted to be able to become self-employed and make enough money to quit his job in the drum department at Trade Up Music. This is the Potato Champion story.

In 2005, Mike was driving around Portland with a friend and potential investor looking for a place that might work for them to open a storefront where they could sell pommes frites. Pommes frites are better known in the United States as French fries. In Belgium and France and other places, they enjoy "pommes frites."

Mike loves music; to him, playing music is a life-giving endeavor. Following high school, Mike spent some time traveling the United States with a band. While on those adventures, he fell in love with pommes frites. He had them in Holland, Belgium, New York City, San Francisco and Vancouver, British Columbia. Mike soon found himself living in Portland, Oregon, and following concerts with his band, he would wish for late-night dining options beyond the iconic (and delicious) Original Hotcake House. Mike would also lament the lack of friteries in Portland. His friend would tell him, "You should open one."

That is how Mike found himself in the spring of 2005 in a car with a friend looking for places to open a friterie. Later that summer, Mike's friend and potential investor pulled out. He wished Mike the best and encouraged him to press on with his dream. Food carts began to catch Mike's eye, and he thought maybe, just maybe, a food cart is the way to go.

## *"My Culinary Experience Began and Ended with Delivering Pizza"*

One of the reasons why food cart owners inspire me so much is because they pursue their dreams, even when conventional wisdom would say that they have little chance of success. Like Johnny Utah leaving the plane without a parachute in hot pursuit of Bodhi in *Point Break*, they just go for it!

Mike was not going to let a little thing like not having any culinary background stop him from opening a food cart that sold pommes frites. Mike began a three-year research program teaching himself to make pommes frites and sauces. He started with a lot of reading, and then eventually he bought a home fryer and started peeling and frying potatoes. He mentioned to me that once the cart opened and he moved from his home fryer to a forty-five-pound fryer, the learning curve started all over again.

Mike said that starting a food cart *was* his culinary school. For a guy whose culinary journey started with delivering pizzas, he has done very well in the cooking department. Today, the sauces and ketchups, and most everything else they sell at Potato Champion, is made from scratch. They even make the peanut butter that goes into the peanut satay sauce.

## Why "Potato Champion"?

Mike struggled with what to call his food cart. "Naming a food cart is as bad as naming a band," he said. Mike began reading about the history of the potato and found his inspiration. He learned that in 1748, the French parliament outlawed the cultivation of potatoes. Potatoes were believed to be dangerous and one of the causes of leprosy. Enter Antoine-Augustin Parmentier. Antoine fought for France in the Seven Years' War, was captured, became a prisoner of war and was put in prison in Prussia. While in prison, Antoine was faced with eating the repugnant hog feed known as potatoes.

The war ended, and Antoine returned home and began studying nutritional chemistry. He began to promote the potato as a safe source of nourishment. In 1772, the Paris Faculty of Medicine declared potatoes safe to eat. The reason that French cuisine includes potatoes is because of Antoine-Augustin Parmentier, the potato champion.

## "I Lived for Three Years Like a Robot on Zombie Mode"

When Potato Champion opened, Mike worked six and seven days a week. That first year, Potato Champion was open from 6:00 p.m. to 3:00 a.m. Back then, the cart was open from Wednesday to Saturday. Mike did the shopping, the books and lots of food prep from Sunday to Tuesday.

Mike spent three years working those six and seven days a week. During this period, with rare exceptions, he had to put his music on the shelf. Mike paid the price that many people who succeed in a startup pay. If you aren't ready for that, don't open a food cart.

## "The Weird Feeling of Sitting Still"

After three years, Mike was able to shift from working in the cart to running the business. This is also when he finally began having regularly scheduled days off. Mike shared how incredibly hard it was to recalibrate a schedule that allowed him to have some breathing room. Yes, Mike worked very hard and put in some crazy hours building his startup. But he said that it was worth it and that he has found the journey to be very satisfying.

## *Changing Portland*

When Mike opened Potato Champion in 2008 at 12th and Hawthorne, most food carts were located across the Willamette River in downtown Portland. Those food carts were also, for the most part, open during lunch, Monday through Friday. Very few, if any, were open for dinner or late-night dining.

Bo Kwon, founder of the KOi Fusion empire, has inspired many people to believe that they could succeed as a food cart owner. Mike McKinnon has inspired many people to believe that they could have a successful Portland food cart that was not downtown.

I know that before Mike opened Potato Champion, there were a handful of successful food cart that were not downtown—the Flavour Spot Food Cart comes to mind. However, I have heard many food cart owners tell me that it was Mike and Potato Champion that inspired them to believe that they could have a successful food cart in Portland located somewhere other than downtown.

Quite a few food carts owners have also told me that it was Mike's example of staying open until 3:00 a.m. that convinced them that they could do more than just lunch.

Mike McKinnon, owner of the Potato Champion Food Cart.

# 3:00 A.M.

Before Mike got to the Cartopia Food Cart Pod on 12ᵗʰ and Hawthorne, the few food carts that were there were open during lunch. Mike started staying open until 3:00 a.m. In doing so, he was fulfilling a dream that he had years ago. Portland now had a late-night friterie!

From the beginning, Mike was very diligent about maintaining his posted hours. Potato Champion would stay open until 3:00 a.m., even if the pod was empty at 1:00 a.m. Back then, other (and now defunct) food carts would close up early on slow nights. Mike persisted with his vision, and a late-night food cart scene was born. Today, all of the Cartopia food carts are open late at night on Fridays and Saturdays.

## The Cartopia Late-Night Dining Scene

The Cartopia late-night scene is a blast. If you haven't been, go! If you are visiting Portland, make sure that you visit Cartopia and do so on a Friday or Saturday night just after midnight. Rain or shine, you can get a great meal and enjoy it in covered seating. Cartopia is the perfect place to end a Friday or Saturday evening in Portland. I tip my food cart hat to Mike McKinnon. He is my potato champion!

*What's Next*: Mike hopes to open up a brick-and-mortar Potato Champion some day. He would be delighted to be able to serve hamburgers to go with his pommes frites. He would also serve Mitraillettes, which Mike first had in Belgium. They are a sandwich commonly available at Belgian friteries and cafés containing meat and pommes frites. Mike has also begun to look into packaging some of his ketchups and sauces for retail sale. He gets many requests to bottle his rosemary truffle ketchup!

*When You Go*: Take a few friends and share at least three orders among yourselves. Get a large order of fries and pick the three sauces that sound most appealing to you. I especially like the horseradish ketchup, the pesto mayo and the rosemary truffle ketchup. Also, get the Pulled Pork Fries—topped with slow-cooked Carlton Farms pork shoulder and Potato Champion's own whiskey barbecue sauce. Lastly, get the PB and J Fries. This is my favorite dish at Potato Champion! Fries topped with Potato Champion's peanut satay sauce and chipotle raspberry sauce. The flavors work so well together.

# WE OPENED THE CART TO SAVE OUR OWN ASSES: BIG-ASS SANDWICH

The Big-Ass Sandwich Food Cart opened on December 21, 2009, and it has become one of Portland's most iconic food carts. The press loves it, celebrities stop by and, in 2013, it expanded from one food cart to two. The Travel Channel's Adam Richman declared that it has the best sandwich in the Northwest. I am thrilled that I get to share Brian and Lisa's startup journey with you.

## *Laid Off...Again*

Brian and Lisa met in February 2003 at the 5 Point in Seattle, Washington, and they have been together ever since. In June 2009, they were living in Portland, and Lisa was laid off for the second time in two years. They realized that because of the economic downturn, Lisa was not going to find another job in her industry. They were going to have to do something to stay afloat.

For almost as long as they have been together, Brian and Lisa had talked about opening a restaurant. Both of them had wanted to be self-employed for many years. When Lisa was a teenager, her parents started their first business, and that inspired Lisa to want to start her own as well some day. Brian has wanted to be self-employed since "the first time the boss unfairly yelled at me for something stupid and ridiculous."

## *Maybe We Could Open a Food Cart*

Right after Lisa was laid off in June 2009, Brian and Lisa decided that it was time to pull the trigger on being self-employed. Starting a restaurant was not in the cards financially, and they began to consider opening a food cart. Brian's one big hesitation for opening a food cart was that he wanted a cart that had a commercial kitchen that he did not have to fight to get to work. Up to this point, Brian had twenty years' experience working in the restaurant business. He started washing dishes at fourteen and worked his way up the culinary ladder. He spent ten of those twenty years working as a chef in fine dining establishments.

Lisa and Brian had been looking at used food carts, but as Brian put it, "The used carts we looked at were hammered to dog #^%@, and the kitchens in them sucked." He added, "The way we found our food cart was both fortuitous and flukish." Brian and Lisa were hanging out with Josh, a chef and a friend of Brian's. An acquaintance of Josh's happened to stop by, and he knew about some guys who were food cart builders. Brian and Lisa met with Rich and Jason, and Brian discovered that he could design his own kitchen.

They met with Rich and Jason a number of times after that. One of these times, they were meeting in a coffee shop on Belmont that Brian and Lisa liked, and Brian asked Rich, "Hey, when are we going to get to see one of your food carts?" Rich said, "Ummm, actually…Your cart is going to be our first one."

Brian and Lisa were lucky enough to be working with the guys who were starting Northwest Mobile Kitchens (NMK). Today, Rich is the owner of NMK, a very good food cart/food truck builder. Incidentally, NMK built a number of the food carts featured in this book, including Potato Champion, PDX Six Seven One and Yolk. The way they found their food cart was indeed fortuitous.

## The Secret Origin of the Big-Ass Sandwich

A few weeks later, Brian and Lisa were in that very same coffee shop talking about the menu for their food cart. Brian wanted something that was unique and tasted great. Then he remembered his days cooking on the line. Some days, you would get a whole ten-minute break to smoke a cigarette and eat enough food to keep going for the next nine to ten hours. It was common to throw everything that you were going to eat— even the French fries—between two pieces of bread so that you could consume it quickly before your ten minutes were up and you had to hop back on the line.

As he was describing this to Lisa, she said, "Brian, you make incredible roast beef and really good cheese sauce. We could take both of those and some French fries and make a sandwich out of them." Brian then held up his hands as if he were holding this sandwich and loudly exclaimed, "This is gonna be a big-ass sandwich!"

Lisa has a friend who told her before they opened the cart that "opening a business together will really test your relationship." Early on, it was very

Brian and Lisa Wood, owners of the Big-Ass Sandwich Food Cart.

hard for Brian and Lisa to figure out how to work well together. It was really tough on their relationship, and they fought a lot. Brian remembered more than once thinking, "What the *&#@ did we do?" Many nights ended with "whiskey fights."

They did gut it out. They pressed on through the adversity and found a rhythm that worked for them. As a couple, they are doing awesome. Spend just fifteen minutes with them, and you can tell that they like each other and that they have done the hard work of building a great relationship. As business partners, they came up with a division of labor that worked for them. In the cart, Brian is in charge; if it is a food question, talk to Brian. Lisa handles the rest. Brian is an excellent chef and prepares wonderful food, while Lisa oversees their social media platforms. She is stellar at it! Lisa uses social media to effectively tell their brand story, and she is very diligent about connecting with the many fans that Big-Ass Sandwich has. "Social media brought the people in, and the food kept them coming back," she noted.

## If You Start a Food Cart, Be Prepared to...

I asked Brian and Lisa what they would tell someone wanting to open a food cart. Lisa's immediate response was, "Don't do it; it is harder that you think." Here is the rest of what they shared with me in rapid-fire succession:

- Be prepared to give up three years of your life.
- Be prepared to work really, really hard.
- Be prepared to be a pauper for a few years.
- Be prepared to give up your summers.
- Be prepared for the struggle.
- And for the love of God, do some marketing!

Brian and Lisa speak very highly of their crew and of the loyal core group of fans they have. They give much credit to the people who have helped them get this far. "We wouldn't have made it this far without our crew and our fans," said Lisa. I applaud the fact that they are sincerely grateful to the people who have stood by them.

## Grit and Guts

Brian shared with me that in his younger years, he always marveled at the people who were able to start their own business. It feels good to now be on that very same journey. He wistfully spoke of people he knew in the past who wanted to start their business and never did. Lisa added, "It takes balls to make that leap." Brian and Lisa, I am one of your fans, and speaking on the behalf of the legion of other supporters you have out there, we applaud the fact that you had the guts to make that leap.

*What's Next*: Brian and Lisa would love to open two brick-and-mortar restaurants. The first one they want to open is a Big-Ass Sandwich restaurant—somewhere people could hear great music, enjoy awesome beer and chow down on a Big-Ass Sandwich. Once that dream has come true, Brian longs to someday open a gastro pub that features rustic comfort food and has a huge fireplace. I wish that you could have seen the look in his eye when he was describing this place to me.

*When You Go*: Get a Big-Ass Roast Beef with extra béchamel, grilled mushrooms and horseradish. I also love the Big-Ass Breakfast Sandwich. I get mine with bacon. The scrambled eggs pair incredibly well with the ciabatta roll and the béchamel. My absolute favorite Big-Ass Sandwich only comes around once a year, at Thanksgiving. The Big-Ass Thanksgiving Sandwich has turkey, fries, homemade gravy and homemade stuffing made with sausage, walnuts, sweet potatoes, rosemary and cranberries. Make sure to get extra, extra turkey gravy. Yes, I said "extra" twice. You will want *lots* of gravy. Once your gravy-laden Big-Ass Thanksgiving Sandwich is handed to you, don't unwrap it. Put it down and let it rest for few minutes. Let the fries absorb that glorious gravy. After about four minutes, unwrap your beauty and be swept away into gravy-bathed Thanksgiving heaven.

# THE BOSS YOU WISH YOU HAD: GRILLED CHEESE GRILL

On April 20, 2009, Matt Breslow opened his first food cart at 11th and Alberta. The Grilled Cheese Grill is a very successful food cart business here in Portland. It has four food carts—three Grilled Cheese Grill locations and the Shot Gun Sub Shop Food Cart. Matt Breslow is the entrepreneur who founded it all, and he is the boss you wish you had.

## Moving to Portland

Matt grew up in New Jersey, and his family visited Portland when he was kid. He had aunts, uncles and cousins here. Matt also spent two consecutive summers here in Portland when he was eleven and twelve years old.

Matt remembered Portland being the place where he felt the most at home. He always assumed that he would move to Portland someday and settle here. That someday came about in the summer of 2007. Matt moved to Portland to open a breakfast place. Matt went to five different Portland restaurants that served breakfast. Screen Door was the fifth. After eating brunch at Screen Door, Matt concluded that "Portland had breakfast covered" and began to look for other culinary endeavors.

Matt Breslow, owner of the Grilled Cheese Grill Food Cart.

## *Three Questions*

Matt then noticed the food cart scene, and he began to wonder if maybe starting a food cart would make sense. Matt had three questions related to starting a food cart. One, what would his cuisine be? Two, where would he put his first food cart? Three, what about the "nine months" of rain?

A little while later, Matt found himself sitting on a couch in his cousin's home. They were both hungry, and in the kitchen was half a loaf of wheat bread, a block of cheese, some turkey, some hummus and an avocado.

Matt and his cousin proceeded to make an eclectic grilled cheese sandwich that was very tasty. Matt began to think, "You know, maybe grilled

The Grilled Cheese Grill's first food cart at 11th and Alberta.

cheese sandwiches would be the way to go." Matt realized that there are lots of different kinds of bread and cheese and that he could use bread and cheese as a palette for being very creative. At the same time, Matt loves comfort food, and he knew that for many people, a grilled cheese sandwich is quintessential comfort food.

Matt was not sure that he wanted to have to start out with a food cart downtown handling the lunch crowd. He was also not sure that a food cart could work somewhere other than downtown. Then Matt began talking to Mike, the founder of the Potato Champion Food Cart. According to Matt, Mike had singlehandedly turned the food cart pod at 12th and Hawthorne (known as Cartopia) into a late-night destination. Matt found Mike to be very helpful and insightful.

Matt decided that he did not have to be downtown to have a successful food cart and that he could serve more than just lunch. He liked the Alberta neighborhood; he found a vacant lot on 11th and decided that a food cart on Alberta might just work.

What about the "nine months" of rain? In a stroke of pure genius, it occurred to Matt that he could put a school bus on the lot next to his food cart, and people could sit inside it when it was raining.

## The Name

All three of Matt's questions had been answered, and now he needed to name his cart. Matt thought through a number of names. He wanted a name that was memorable and clear. He did not want anyone to have to wonder about what it was he was selling at his food cart. He wanted a name that would be good for word of mouth. The name Grilled Cheese Grill fit the bill on all accounts.

I have to say that I love Grilled Cheese Grill's motto: "So come by for a taste of your childhood. Unless your childhood sucked, and then we'll let ya have a taste of ours." That tagline always makes me chuckle, and as a survivor of a very rough boyhood myself, I appreciate the playful and caring acknowledgement that not everyone looks back fondly on their childhood.

## Extend Your Food Cart Brand

Matt has expanded his Grilled Cheese Grill startup into a thriving enterprise that has four food carts, a school bus and a double-decker bus.

I very much believe that food cart owners need to extend their brand somehow—start selling branded merchandise like A Cajun Life, add more carts like KOi Fusion and Fried Egg I'm in Love or go brick-and-mortar like former food cart Lardo. You can only sell so much from one food cart. If most food cart owners are going to achieve the better life they wanted when they launched their startup, they are going to have to expand some way, somehow.

If you are going to grow your food cart business from one food cart to two or more food carts, you have to transition from being the person cooking the food and interacting with most of your customers to successfully hiring and then leading a team of employees who will do most of the cooking and interact with most of your customers.

## Hiring and Leading Employees

Successfully hiring and then leading team of employees is a whole different set of skills from those needed to start a food cart, and Matt Breslow has mastered these skills. I believe that the mindset and perspective that Matt has about hiring and leading employees has greatly contributed to the success of Grilled Cheese Grill. Said Matt, "90 percent of finding a good employee is hiring."

Grilled Cheese Grill has a very interesting job application. (You can Google "Grilled Cheese Grill job application" to see it.) The most important part to Matt are the six questions. Matt particularly likes question #5 ("Please describe your last good argument") and question #1 ("Please describe either your favorite or least favorite job").

Matt feels that how someone answers the six questions on his job application will reveal how well someone communicates, and it will also tell whether or not they are a complainer and a whiner. Matts wants employees who are good communicators because they will most likely be talking to his customers.

## Morale Is Key

Matt does not want employees who are complainers because food carts are small and, as he put it, "Who wants to spend eight hours in a small space with a whiner and a complainer?" Morale is a *big* deal to Matt. "Morale is the biggest thing a business owner should be concerned with. Bad morale can spread faster that a virus." Speaking about morale, Matt went on to say, "Work is not always fun, and maintaining good morale helps the people who work for you to actually want to come to work."

Matt has worked in a number of corporate settings, and he has seen firsthand how much poor morale negatively effects productivity and the bottom line. He went on to make two powerful statements that I have been reflecting on ever since I first heard them. "My most important job is to treat my staff well and keep them happy and make sure that they look forward to coming for work…I care about my staff more than I care about my customers. I care about my staff so that they will care about my customers."

I have had a number of "bosses'" in my lifetime, and after interviewing Matt for this book, I realized that very few of them had the kind of mindset toward me that Matt has to his staff. I also realized that I would really enjoy working for someone with Matt's perceptive.

*What's Next*: Matt is planning on adding a mobile food cart in 2014 so that the Grilled Cheese Grill can do events and add catering to the mix. Matt is also looking at adding a Grilled Cheese Grill brick-and-mortar restaurant sometime in the next year or two. He would love to have a place where people could get French fries with their grilled cheese sandwiches; he would also serve breakfast there. My best guess is that Matt's first brick-and-mortar Grilled Cheese Grill would be like a wonderful old-school diner, breakfast in the morning and grilled cheese creations for lunch and dinner.

*When You Go*: First, get the Kindergartner. It's a classic grilled cheese sandwich. Don't you dare get wheat bread or cheddar! A proper classic grilled cheese sandwich has white bread and American cheese. Next, get yourself a Cheesus, a delightful cheeseburger. Instead of a bun, you get two distinctive grilled cheese sandwiches bookending a ⅓-pound burger, with lettuce, tomato, ketchup and mustard. One of the grilled cheese sandwiches on the Cheesus is made with pickles and American cheese, and the other is made with grilled onions and Colby jack. Please note: I add avocado to my Cheesus. I grew up near Fallbrook, California, and I love avocado on a burger.

# CAPTIVATED BY PORTLAND WHILE WALKING ACROSS THE STEEL BRIDGE: WHIFFIES PIES

Gregg Abbott opened the Whiffies Fried Pies Food Cart in March 2009. Gregg grew up in Upstate New York and gradated from Lyme Central High School. Barry Davis is now the principal at Lyme Central, and back in the day, he was Gregg's social studies teacher. Mr. Davis remembered Gregg and shared that he was a very smart student.

From there, Gregg went on to attend Evergreen State College in Olympia, Washington, and when he finished school, he got on a Greyhound bus and came to Portland to see a former girlfriend who had moved here. He left the bus terminal midday and walked across the Broadway Bridge, checking the city out on foot.

Gregg remembered walking back over the Steel Bridge just at dusk, stopping on the bridge and looking out across the water. Gregg said that it was right then, standing on that bridge, that he became captivated by Portland. The longer Gregg lived in Portland, the more he liked it. "Portland was like a city version of Evergreen," he noted.

Gregg fondly remembered "that sense of wonder you get when you first come to Portland." He found Portland to be like a huge, citywide performance art production, and he was excited to become one of the performers. Gregg believes that Portland is a place where you can do your own thing and make something of yourself.

## I Can Do That: Inspired by Food Carts

Gregg had wanted to open food cart of his own for eight years before he opened Whiffies. For a time, he had a job working downtown, and he used to have lunch at the Honkin' Big Burrito Food Cart and at the Divine Café Food Cart. Gregg remembered thinking, "I can do that. I could open a food cart and be in business for myself."

While Gregg was growing up, his parents ran a catering company out of the family home, and Gregg got an insider's view into what it takes to succeed in the food industry. Gregg's dad was the chef, and his mom handled the books and the marketing.

## This Is a Bad Idea

Finally, it was time to move ahead with his long-held dream of self-employment. Gregg found a food cart for sale on Craigslist and went to Seattle to pick it up. He met the couple and paid for the cart, and as he was hooking it up to the truck to haul it back to Portland, it started snowing. Gregg told himself, "This is a bad idea." The winters he spent in Upstate New York paid off, and he made it home just fine.

## Fried Pies

Greg wanted to make something that was easy to prepare and delicious to eat. He wanted to offer gourmet fair food. Gregg noticed that no one was offering hand-held fried pies, and he and his father, Dion, began to perfect recipes and figure out the menu.

## It Was an Inside Joke

Gregg and his dad, who is also a restaurant consultant, had an inside joke between them. Neither of them likes overpriced dishes that are insubstantial—"Like when a chef puts three spoonfuls on a plate and sells it for fifty dollars." They called those kind of meals "Whiffies."

Gregg felt that his fried pies were going to offer people good food for a good value—they would be anything but "Whiffies." His dad once asked him, "What are you going to name your food cart?" Gregg answered back, mostly teasing, "Whiffies." When it came time to fill out the business paperwork and put down an actual name, Gregg chose Whiffies. He needed a name right then, and that is what came to mind.

Gregg Abbott, owner of the Whiffies Fried Pies Food Cart.

## 12<sup>th</sup> and Hawthorne

Gregg had been to Potato Champion and loved it. He was convinced that his soon-to-be-open food cart would do very well there. Gregg called up the landlord and said, "I am opening up a food cart, and Mike with Potato Champion says that I should put my cart at 12<sup>th</sup> and Hawthorne." The landlord replied, "Well, if Mike says that you should be here, you are in." Later, when Gregg actually got to know Mike, he shared that story with him, and Mike got quite a chuckle out of it. Food cart owners do what they have to do to make it work.

Gregg has done well with his business, and it has been good to him. Gregg even met his future wife, Claire, at Whiffies. She came to the cart in 2009 for her birthday, met Gregg and subsequently sent him a message on Facebook. Greg saw that she had been posting pictures of food on her Facebook page, and he messaged her back on Facebook and suggested that they go out to dinner sometime—they could both take pictures of the meal.

The next time you are near 12<sup>th</sup> and Hawthorne, stop by and get yourself a Whiffies fried pie.

*What's Next*: Gregg is planning to get a second food cart so that he can cater events. He gets a number of requests to have a Whiffies Food Cart come to events.

*When You Go*: There are so many good options! I love the barbecue brisket and the chicken pot pie. On the sweet side, I am very fond of the peach, the Oregon mixed berry combo and the "Mounds" (coconut pudding and chocolate).

*Recipes*: You can find a Whiffies recipes in the *Food Truck Cookbook* by John T. Edge.

# *Food Writer's Perspective:*
## JEANNA BARRETT

Jeanna Barrett is the founder and chief dater at 50 Food Truck Dates (the50dates.com), a site about modern dating amid the national food truck craze. Jeanna goes on blind and "real" dates with men to food trucks in cities across the nation and then writes afterward about the date and the food. Part food blog and part dating rag, Jeanna hopes to simultaneously find love and not gain twenty-five pounds from street food. Through her project, she's also launched National Food Truck Date Day (February 14), a movement to change the negative sentiment around Valentine's Day. She resides in San Francisco by way of Seattle, but her food truck travels have taken her to Portland, Austin, New York City, Boston, Chicago, LA and Philadelphia. Where there are food trucks and/or guys, you can find her.

I first visited Portland's food truck scene in May 2013, ten years after the last time I had stumbled into Portland in my early twenties to stay at a two-story dive motel near the Doug Fir, where I cheers-ed a man in a bathrobe grilling hot dogs in the parking lot and sang Journey's "Don't Stop Believin'" at the top of my lungs through the Pearl District. To say my 2013 trip was different is an understatement, yet it was still hilariously similar to grilling hot dogs in a parking lot. This time, nearly a decade later, I came to eat my way through one of the more famous foundations of our nation's street food scene.

When I was twenty-one, the food cart scene in Portland was in its infant stages—something I didn't notice or hear about while walking the streets of the City of Roses. Now Portland's street food has grown into something so famous that it was my first chosen stop on a series of "food truck pilgrimages" I had planned in half a dozen of our nation's cities. My plan for these pilgrimages was to taste every food truck morsel I could possibly fit into a long weekend, coupled with a taste of the city's dating scene.

I landed in Portland during a gray and drizzly May morning, and my baby sister picked me up so we could immediately start to tackle my list of more than twenty food carts I hoped to squeeze into four days of meals. We drove down

SE Hawthorne in search of Fried Egg I'm in Love, my first chosen Portland food cart. I've been a huge virtual fan of the cart since stumbling across its account on Twitter because I love puns, breakfast sandwiches and the Cure. (Yes, social media is super important for food carts, otherwise traveling food writers like little ol' me wouldn't know about them!)

We saw food carts poking out on nearly every corner we drove by, and as I pointed and shouted, "There's one! There's one over there!" my sister exclaimed, "It's like a mini treasure hunt!" Yes, driving around to find one of Portland's best food carts really is like a treasure hunt.

Once we had moved to downtown for a food cart lunch, I was struck by the sheer number of carts that inhabit each corner of Portland. The city has truly been transformed by the pods and blocks of stationary carts painted in bright colors, often paired with picnic tables and community spaces. While very different from San Francisco's food truck scene, where the food is served in full-sized trucks that roam the city, always changing location, I love how Portland has built vibrant, intriguing food cart pod communities found everywhere throughout the city and has turned food carts into a way of life in the Pacific Northwest. My very favorite "pod" is located at 23rd and Alberta, which even features a beer cart to wash a drink down with your cart meal (beer and food is the best choice for dates).

During my Portland culinary cart exploration, which included eating at nine food trucks in the first day, I found that while the number of food carts in Portland shows years and depth of street food knowledge that far surpasses many of America's cities, there are still a number of mediocre "roach coach" carts throughout the city. But take the time to do a little research and make special trips to each of Portland's pods, and you'll find more than a few hidden food cart gems as you explore. Here are some of my favorites.

Vada Holes from Tiffin Asha: I was able to snag a visit to Tiffin Asha during the first week it was open thanks to Steven, and I fell in love with food cart owner and chef Elizabeth Golay's south Indian food. Since most of the Indian food you'll eat in Indian restaurants is from northern India, southern Indian food is a unique little treat not to be missed. As a fan of sweet and savory, I was *obsessed* with Tiffin Asha's Vada Holes—a savory dal donut rolled in coconut-chili fleur de sel and served with sambar. The donut is warm and chewy, as well as perfectly spicy and sweet. They're served in orders of five and eight vadas, but really I wanted twenty-four, so I recommend starting out with four orders of the large vada holes. Don't mistrust an expert.

Black Pepper Dumplings (Khinkali) from Kargi Gogo: If I tell you that Kargi Gogo serves Georgian food, do you think peach pie, barbecue and sweet tea? Think again. Kargi Gogo is authentic Georgian street food from the Republic of Georgia, and the cart owners Sean and McKinze know how to cook it because they spent two years there while volunteering for the Peace Corps. The story of how the cart came to be is interesting; however, I was most intrigued by the steaming salt-and-pepper dumplings that were being handed out their cart window. There's no shortage of dumplings in different cuisines across the world, but the heavily black-peppered dumplings from Georgia are something different and special. So moist is the meat inside that it's actually swimming in juices and is better eaten upside down, holding the top of the dumpling like an upside-down top. First bite a hole in the dumpling and then suck the juices out and finish off the dumpling in an incredible spinning circle of spiced dough.

Chicken and Rice from Nong's Khao Man Gai: I feel like Nong's Khao Man Gai (or, simply, Chicken and Rice) is synonymous with talking about the success and deliciousness of Portland's food cart scene. Often called one of the most popular food carts, the chicken and rice dish is an unsuspecting treat, and if you only had one hour and one food cart to visit in Portland, I'd tell you to go now, run, to Nong's. When I first received the brown paper bag from a tall, loud and somewhat strange man who said to me, "Today is the 144th day of the year!" as I approached the cart window, I didn't know what to expect. Could anything sound more boring than "chicken and rice"? When you unwrap the white butcher paper, you'll find rice, chicken breast, a few slices of cucumber, pieces of cilantro and a little side cup of sauce. Pour the sauce all over the chicken and rice, stir and prepare to have your mind blown. I have no idea what's in that sauce, but it is by far one of the more exploding mouthfuls of flavor experiences I have ever had. From ginger to lemongrass to chilies, I couldn't place my finger on the dozens of flavors, but I knew that I wanted to eat that chicken and rice dish one hundred times over. You can even buy bottles of the sauce Nong makes now at the cart and specialty stores throughout Portland to bring home a little piece of Nong's Khao Man Gai to your kitchen, which I did. Two bottles in my usually-never-checked suitcase.

Naughty in Nogales Tater Tots from Timber's Doghouse PDX: Often when I think of street food, I think of the greasiest comfort food that makes your mouth water and your belly ache. Who doesn't love a burger, hot dog or fries smothered and covered in cheese and gravy? Even better, who wouldn't love a big serving of tater tots, smothered and covered in jalapenos, grilled onions, pineapple, bacon, pepper jack cheese and spicy sauce, all served up in a dog bowl? The Naughty in Nogales Tater Tot bowl from Timber's is literally the messiest, dirtiest, spiciest, creamiest and naughtiest pile of salty comfort food that you'll ever need to order before you can die happy. You're welcome.

The FoPo Christo from the Egg Carton: I'm a huge fan of breakfast foods and bacon, so I was over the moon to hear about all the different breakfast food carts located throughout Portland—so much so that I did my own miniature breakfast food cart tour while visiting. Again, being a huge fan of sweet and savory dishes, I fell in love with the FoPo Christo from the Egg Carton, which is an amazing combo of sweet and salty breakfast foods. The FoPo Christo is a twist on a Monte Cristo—an oozy fried egg, bacon, Canadian bacon, cheddar cheese, spicy mustard and strawberry jam between two slices of French toast. A perfect food cart start to a Pacific Northwest morning.

# PART II
# WE MOVED TO PORTLAND
# TO OPEN A FOOD CART

## WE MOVED FROM FLORENCE, ITALY, TO PORTLAND, OREGON, TO OPEN A FOOD CART: BURRASCA

"I have a friend who is moving from Italy to Portland to open a food cart. Would you be willing to meet with him and help him?" I was asked that question on April 29, 2013. I love a good story, and that sounded like a great one. The thing that amuses me to no end is that I was at the Italian Market Food Cart when I was asked that question. I am always amazed at how the dots connect.

In the fall of 2012, Erin and Andrew, owners of the Italian Market Food Cart, had a successful Kickstarter campaign. One of the pledge amounts allowed you to shave Andrew's head as a prize. A good friend of theirs, Rob, happily made that pledge so that he could see Andrew sheared like a sheep in the spring.

Rob lives in Philly, so I was asked to come over and remove all of Andrew's hair. If you Google "The Shaving Food Cart TV YouTube," you can watch the fun eight-minute short that my friend Ken Wilson made to commemorate this event.

Shaving a food cart owner is hard work. To recover, I got an Ellsworth from the Italian Market and headed into the Belmont Station to enjoy a beer

Paolo Calamai, owner of the Burrasca Food Cart.

with my beef brisket reward. I was enjoying great food and great beer and having a wonderful time. Then I was asked if I would meet with someone name Paolo, who was moving from Italy to Portland to open a food cart. I handed over one of my business cards and enthusiastically said, "Yes, I would be delighted to. When Paolo gets to America, have him call me."

## Lunch with Paolo

A short while later, I got a phone call from someone who identified himself as Paolo Calamai. As soon as I heard him say his name, I immediately flashed back to that day at the Italian Market Food Cart. I couldn't wait to meet Paolo and hear his story.

Paolo and I met at the Carte Blanche Food Cart on June 27, 2013. We shared a meal, and I got to hear a little bit of Paolo's hopes and dreams. His passion was palpable, and I knew right then that his still embryonic food cart would be very successful.

As we visited, I provided Paolo with some pro bono food cart consulting. We chatted about menus, possible names for his food cart, branding, social media and more. As I drove away from that meeting, I was filled with anticipation about what he and his lovely wife, Elizabeth, would develop.

## The Food at Burrasca Is Off the Charts

Paolo has been cooking since he was a small child. In his youth, he spent many hours in the kitchen with his mama and nonna (grandma), learning how make the dishes he now serves at Burrasca. Each day that Burrasca is open, Paolo makes his own bread, one of the many things he learned long ago while standing on a stepstool in that Florence kitchen.

The last week of August 2013, Burrasca opened, and I finally got to sample Paolo's cuisine. Most of the dishes left me speechless. Paolo grew up in Florence, Italy, and Burrasca focuses on the food he grew up with. You can get dishes that are common to both the city of Florence and the region of Tuscany.

One of my favorites dishes at Burrasca is the Arista alla Fiorentina—a roasted pork loin made with fennel pollen. Cooking with fennel pollen is something Paolo picked up from Dario Cecchini, a world-renowned butcher who, like Paolo, is also from Tuscany. What Paolo does with pork is masterful. The pork is tender, rich with flavor and perfectly seasoned.

Another amazing dish that you can get at Burrasca is Inzimino, a Florentine dish made with squid and spinach that has been simmered in red wine and herbs. Yep, you can get squid at a Portland food cart, and it is exquisite.

## *Paolo Fell in Love with the United States*

Paolo first came to America for a vacation in 1984. He fell in love with the United States. He remembered being impressed with the open spaces, the national parks, the freedom and the sense that opportunity abounded. To Paolo, America was the place where people could successfully pursue their dreams.

A few years later found Paolo living in San Francisco, working the front of the house in a restaurant there. It was in San Francisco in 1992 that Paolo met and fell in love with Elizabeth Petrosian. Their first date was to a winery for a picnic.

Eventually, Paolo and Elizabeth married and moved to Florence, Italy, where they started a family and had two beautiful children.

## *A Long-Held Dream to Open a Restaurant*

Since his early twenties, Paolo has wanted to own his own restaurant. This is a dream that has been smoldering in his heart for many years. One of his biggest obstacles to this dream was that Paolo did not have the financial resources needed to do such a thing.

In the summer of 2011, Paolo and Elizabeth came to Portland for a vacation because they had dear friends who were living here. While they were here, they checked out the Portland food cart scene, and Paolo began to wonder about the possibility of maybe opening his own cart there. Upon returning home to Florence, Paolo and Elizabeth began researching what it would take to do just that.

By the end of the fall of 2011, they had decided that they were going to move across the globe and come to Portland to open a food cart so that Paolo could begin pursing his dream of owning a restaurant. They began the process of selling both their home in Florence and many of their possessions. They were going to invest these proceeds.

## *Leaving Florence*

Their last night in Florence, June 16, 2013, Paolo and Elizabeth were robbed by bandits using sleeping gas. They woke up to find that the small amount of jewelry they had—jewelry with deep sentimental value—had been stolen.

They discovered that their wedding rings been taken off their fingers while they were knocked out. Elizabeth teared up when she talked about this incident and how violated she felt.

## The Name

In Italian, *burrasca* means sea storm. This definition is very evident when you Google "burrasca images."

Burrasca is also the name of the main character in a much-beloved Tuscan children's book written in 1907 and 1908 by Luigi Bertelli under the pen name "Vamba." Paolo and Elizabeth named their food cart Burrasca in honor of this precocious fictional boy who, like Paolo, loves Pappa al Pomodoro, a traditional thick Tuscan soup made with bread and tomatoes. And yes, you can occasionally get Pappa al Pomodoro at Burrasca.

Burrasca. I love that name. It just works. To me it sounds very Italian and very interesting.

The Burrasca Food Cart.

## Bone Tired and Very Happy

Paolo now has the joy that comes from finally being able to pursue a dream that he had held in his heart for a long time. He puts in many long days, working between ten and twelve hours each workday. Paolo comes home from the cart "bone tired" but "very happy." Elizabeth says it is wonderful to see Paolo so fulfilled.

I am just one of the many Burrasca fans who are very glad that Paolo and Elizabeth moved from Florence to Portland to open a food cart.

*What's Next*: For Paolo and Elizabeth, the dream is to see the Burrasca Food Cart become a brick-and-mortar restaurant. They have established a wonderful brand, and I believe that they will make it. I am not alone in this opinion. In October 2013, I was lucky enough to take John and Rita Duyn and Wendy Trunick from Carlton Farms on a food cart tour one beautiful Sunday afternoon. Our food cart adventure took us to four food cart pods, and we ate at seven different carts. John loved the food so much at Burrasca that we "ran the menu." John was blown away by the food. Paolo uses Carlton Farms pork at his cart, and I had asked Paolo to make us Arista alla Fiorentina. Many times, John has eaten Carlton Farms pork that has been prepared at some of Portland's best restaurants by the city's best chefs. John proclaimed that Paolo's pork loin was some the best that he has ever tasted. John visited extensively with Paolo, asking about his story and listening to his hopes and dreams. When our adventure was over and we were in the car, John spoke very enthusiastically about Paolo: "[He] is going to make it. He has what it takes to succeed as a restaurant owner."

*When You Go*: Burrasca, like the Cheese Plate PDX, has a seasonal menu. Every single item I have had at Burrasca has been stunning. Regardless of what is on the menu, just order the dishes that speak to you. Get at least two dishes. It will be some of the best food you have ever had. Of the dishes that I enjoy, my favorites include the Arista alla Fiorentina, the Pappa al Pomodoro, the Pappardelle al Cinghiale (handmade pasta and wild boar) and Crespelle (crepes filled with spinach and ricotta and topped with a béchamel-tomato sauce).

# PLAY THE *ROCKY* MUSIC: THE ITALIAN MARKET

*We moved here for this, and this is our life. We aren't just doing this over the summer, and we aren't doing this part time. We are all in with this cart.*
*—Andrew Vidulich*

Erin Callahan and Andrew Vidulich opened the Italian Market on March 27, 2013, seven grueling months from when they had first expected to open it. Andrew and Erin met in 2010 at the Plough and Stars, Philadelphia's premier Irish pub. Soon they became a couple, and they discovered that both of them wanted to be self-employed. Erin had visited Portland during the summer in her college years to see friends. Erin took Andrew to Portland in 2010 and again in 2011. He loved Portland—the beer, how clean it was and the slower pace.

## We Can Do This

They visited food carts during their first trip to Portland. During their second trip, in 2011, they went to see if maybe they could open a food cart. They visited a number of food carts and even took a very helpful food cart tour with Brett Burmeister. When they got back to Philly, they said, "Let's do it!" They began to work to come up with the funds to have a food cart built. Erin took all the extra shifts she could, and Andrew got a second job.

## The Nightmare Begins

In March 2012, they sent a food cart builder $9,500. They were to pick up their food cart at the beginning of September and pay the remaining $1,000 then. An empty shell of a small trailer was going to have a working commercial kitchen, with all appliances installed, as well as doors, service windows and so on. Over the summer, they were able to secure a spot in a downtown pod to put their cart.

On Thursday, August 30, Andrew and Erin's possessions left Philly in a truck headed for Portland. On Friday night, they had a goodbye dinner with family, and by Saturday morning, September 1, they were getting on a plane and moving to Portland to pursue their dream. They even had a house in Portland rented in which to live.

## 2,865 Miles Away

Early on Friday morning, August 31, everything came crashing down. The phone rang at 5:00 a.m. It was their food cart builder calling to say that she was going out of business and that Andrew and Erin had until 5:00 p.m. at the end of the month to pick up the shell of their unfinished food cart. There was so much bad news to process: the cart was unfinished...*that day* was the last day of the month...and they were in Philadelphia, more than 2,800 miles away.

Thankfully, Erin and Andrew had friends in Portland, Mike and Don, who had a truck with a hitch. The guys went and picked up the shell and put it in the driveway of Andrew and Erin's new Portland home. Andrew remembered being sick to his stomach on Friday night as friends and family were telling him goodbye and wishing them luck with their new business.

On Saturday, September 1, Andrew, Erin, James Brown and Frank Sinatra (their dog and cat) arrived in Portland. Their unfinished food cart was in the driveway. The money they had earned to finish it was gone, and they had no jobs. Welcome to Portland.

> *The world ain't all sunshine and rainbows. It's a very mean and nasty place, and I don't care how tough you are—it will beat you to your knees and keep you there permanently if you let it. You, me or nobody is gonna hit as hard as life. But it ain't about how hard ya hit. It's about how hard you can get hit and keep moving forward—how much you can take and keep moving forward. That's how winning is done.*
>
> —*Rocky Balboa (Sylvester Stallone)*

Andrew and Erin kept battling for their dream. On Tuesday morning, September 4, Andrew hit the streets to find a job. He went into more than one hundred restaurants looking for a job. He kept hearing "summer is over and we have entered our slow season." He kept at it and eventually found a job, as did Erin.

## Kickstarter

Andrew and Erin decided that they would do a Kickstarter to raise the funds to get their empty shell of trailer turned into a food cart. With no training in film and using the software that came with her computer, Erin made a Kickstarter video and submitted their project. Kickstarter approved their project, and it was scheduled to begin on October 22, 2012, and run until November 12, 2012.

They had twenty-one days to get strangers in Portland and friends and family on the East Coast to donate $11,000 so they could get their food cart opened. It felt awkward and uncomfortable to them to ask for assistance; however, they did not want to wait a year to once again work double jobs and save up the needed funds a second time.

## Superstorm Sandy

On October 29, eight days into the Italian Market Kickstarter, Superstorm Sandy made landfall on the East Coast. The Plough and Stars Pub in Philly had a fundraiser for Erin and Andrew scheduled during its October 31 Halloween party. That party got cancelled. Erin and Andrew had thought that they would get most of their pledges from the East Coast. They had only been in Portland seven weeks, and they did not really know many people here. They kept moving forward.

## Rocky Balboa and Vince Papale

I asked Erin and Andrew how they kept going through all of these challenges. They told me that that between the day they arrived in Portland and the day seven months later when they opened their food cart, they watched two movies over and over again: *Rocky* and *Invincible*. Those two inspiring Philly stories kept them going, especially through the first two weeks of their Kickstarter project. They told me that through all of the tough times, they would play the *Rocky* music, keep going and keep battling.

Erin Callahan and Andrew Vidulich, owners of the Italian Market Food Cart.

## Dreams Do Come True

In spite of the second-costliest hurricane in U.S. history, friends and family back east did come through. The Plough and Stars rescheduled the fundraiser and helped out. Local media here in Portland found the story of this courageous couple and helped spread the word. Strangers in Portland did contribute. By November 12, their Kickstarter had raised $12,765. They made it. On March 27, 2013, the Italian Market opened for business.

## The Cuisine

Erin and Andrew proclaimed in their Kickstarter that "cheesesteaks are for tourists." They wanted to bring the best of the Italian food they loved in south Philly to Portland. They were inspired by places like Dinic's, John's Roast Pork and Paesano's. They did share that if you are going to go to Philly and you want to get a cheesesteak, go to Steve's Prince of Steaks.

## *Paying the Price*

The first four months that the Italian Market was open, Erin and Andrew worked seven days a week from 8:00 a.m. to midnight. Food cart owners are a special breed, and they do what it takes to make it happen. Erin and Andrew are great people who own one of Portland's best food carts. I highly encourage you to give them a visit.

*What's Next*: Andrew and Erin hope to some day open up an Italian Market brick-and-mortar Philly-style sandwich shop. The very next step they want to tackle is doing more catering. They get a number of catering requests from people who have loved their take on south Philly food.

*When You Go*: Everything on the menu is wonderful, even the Passyunk, which is an eggplant sandwich suitable for vegetarians. I particularly love the Ellsworth (an Italian beef brisket sandwich), Uncle Mike's Meatball Sub, the Tasker (a Panzanella salad with crusty bread, tomatoes, cart-made mozzarella, fresh basil, onion, cucumber, olive oil and balsamic) and the pretzels. If you get a pretzel, get it "wit" Cheez Whiz.

*Recipes*: You can find two of the Italian Market recipes (Uncle Mike's Meatball Sub; and the Wet Pretzel, a Philly soft pretzel) in *Trailer Food Diaries Cookbook*, Portland edition, vol. 2.

# WE BRING THE CIRCUS TO YOUR DOOR: RETROLICIOUS

Roy and Kimmy Swope opened the Retrolicious Food Cart in May 2012. Most of Portland's food carts stay in one place and are not mobile. Roy and Kimmy's journey, though, has led them to have one of Portland's few mobile food carts.

## *Curry Chicken Salad*

Roy and Kimmy Swope met in Phoenix, Arizona, where they fell in love and became a couple. Together, the two of them, both chefs who have been to culinary school, operated the Paper Plate Café located in the Arizona Republic building in downtown Phoenix.

Roy's curry chicken salad became the most popular dish at the Paper Plate Café. People would call and ask if they were going to be serving the curry chicken salad. If they happened to go several days in a row without preparing the much-loved salad, people would complain vociferously. Roy got to the place where he wondered if he would ever make anything else again.

"I had such good food out of those carts, I thought to myself, 'What a great entrepreneurial opportunity.' It intrigued me and I thought, 'We can do this,'" said Kimmy. The day after Christmas 2010, Roy and Kimmy came to Portland for a vacation. They stayed at Hotel Lucia for a week. As they were out walking around, they saw some food carts, and Kimmy was drawn to them. She said to Roy, inquisitively pointing at one, "What is that?" Every day of their vacation, they ate at food carts.

Phoenix had been good to Roy and Kimmy, and they had enjoyed their time there. Now they were ready for a change. Kimmy wanted rain. She was tired of the heat and the brown. Once they returned back to Phoenix from their vacation, Kimmy told Roy in her ever-so-sweet voice, "I am moving to Portland, and you are invited to join me."

By the fall of 2011, they had decided to move to the Northwest to open a food cart, and they left Phoenix in January 2012—only one year after that fateful vacation.

## The Vagabond Diner in Corvallis

Roy and Kimmy had decided that they would renovate a 1957 Century trailer, call it the Vagabond Diner Food Cart and open it in Corvallis, Oregon. They were then offered free housing at a ranch out in Lacomb, Oregon, a small community about thirty miles east of Corvallis. They left Phoenix and headed for Lacomb.

In short order, they discovered two things: It was going cost too much to renovate the 1957 Century trailer into a food cart, and you can't really operate a food cart in Corvallis. Time to change plans. They found someone to build them a food cart and began looking for a pod in Portland in which to put it.

## Drinking Wine and Playing Gin

While they waited for their new food cart to be built, Roy and Kimmy would sit in the dining room of their Lacomb home, drink wine, play gin and talk about what they would name this new cart. For them, the name Vagabond Diner was attached the Century trailer, and if they weren't going to use that trailer, they weren't going to use the name they had given it.

They decided that they wanted to cook what they called "old-school comfort food." They wanted it to be retro and delicious. As they talked about those concepts, they hit on the name Retrolicious. That name fit exactly with the brand story they wanted to tell.

## On the Road

In May 2012, they opened Retrolicious at a Portland food cart pod. There was one big challenge: they still lived in Lacomb, Oregon. While Lacomb had only been thirty miles from Corvallis, it was eighty miles from Portland.

For the next three months, they drove an hour and forty-five minutes each way to their food cart. They did this five and sometimes six days a week. Moving from Lacomb to Beaverton in August was a huge relief. As they approached their first winter and things started slowing down at the pod, Roy and Kimmy began looking for opportunities to take their food cart to places where people were because they weren't at that pod.

They ended up pulling out of the food cart pod and heading to business parks and large corporations to sell lunch to the employees, who were more than ready to try the new food cart that was coming to them. Every new food cart owner needs a viable game plan to survive the first winter, and Roy and Kimmy had found theirs. They did put the Retrolicious Food Cart back into a pod the next spring; however, by the middle of summer, they discovered that they liked being mobile. They ended up leaving that pod as well.

## Your Fingernails Are Never Painted

Occasionally, I get asked about culinary school. I talked with Roy and Kimmy about this. They both graduated culinary school, they worked in restaurants as employees, they owned a brick-and-mortar restaurant and they now had a successful food cart business.

My first question was, "Should someone work in a restaurant before they attend culinary school?" Both Roy and Kimmy emphatically believe that if you think you might want to go to culinary school in order to pursue a career cooking professionally, work in a restaurant first, even if you have to start out in the dish pit. Kimmy shared, "It is not glamorous. People without a professional cooking background watch the Food Network and think that cooking is a glamorous profession. It is hard work, at times exhausting; your fingernails are never painted…It is one thing to like to cook at home for family and friends; it is quite another to enjoy cooking professionally and doing it ten hours or more a day, day after day."

## Salt Is an Algorithm

I then asked Roy and Kimmy whether they thought that someone should attend culinary school before opening a food cart. They were quick to say that many times they have enjoyed amazing food at food carts owned by people who did not attend culinary school.

That being said, they both noted that if at all possible, a person would do very well to attend a "good" culinary school, especially if you have plans to grow your food cart business beyond just one cart. Roy explained:

> A good culinary school teaches many, many things that you don't learn watching the cooking channel—mother sauces, how to layer flavors, helpful culinary history.
>
> People forget that a food cart is a business. The fewer times you need to touch food before your serve it, the quicker you can get it out to the table and the more profitable you are. Culinary school teaches you systems and fundamentals that allow you to cook more efficiently.
>
> It is one thing to cook a dish for four people; it a different thing altogether to scale up a recipe to make it for forty people or four hundred people or two thousand people. You learn how to scale up recipes in culinary school.
>
> Take salt, for instance. If a recipe that produces four servings calls for a teaspoon of salt, you do not use ten teaspoons of salt when you scale that recipe up to make forty servings. Salt, like a number of ingredients, does not get used in an exponentially linear fashion as you scale up a recipe. Salt is an algorithm.

## *Being Mobile in Portland*

We do not have what I call a "food truck" culture in Portland. The vast majority of our food carts can be found in the same place day after day, and their customers go to them.

Roy and Kimmy, on the other hand, show up where you are. Four to five days a week, they can be found serving lunch at a business park or at a large corporation. They have settled into a mostly regular schedule. For example, their current schedule has them at Nike every Tuesday and at Xerox every Wednesday.

They also provide the food at a number of upscale corporate cocktail parties, and they do lots of weddings. It is common for people to decide that they would love to have a food cart come to their wedding and cater it. It is then that they discover that most Portland food carts are not mobile, and the cart you want may not be able to come to your wedding. That is why a number of food cart owners are looking at getting a second cart that they can use for events.

Roy and Kimmy Swope, owners of the Retrolicious Food Cart.

When Roy and Kimmy cater a wedding, they love to ask about dishes that would invoke good memories for the family. Given their extensive culinary background, Roy and Kimmy are able customize a menu that fits your wedding and your family.

## The Circus Has Come to Town

When Kimmy was a child, she experienced the joy of the circus coming to her town. It was not always there, but when it rolled into town, you went to see it before it moved on to its next stop. When Retrolicious arrives at a business park that it has not been to since last week, and they open their window to see a line of people ten deep waiting to order, her heart swells with gratitude. Now she has the joy of being the one who brings the circus to town.

*What's Next*: Roy and Kimmy can imagine someday opening a small, intimate brick-and-mortar restaurant where you could get a glass of wine with one of Roy's amazing entrées. I wish that they would bottle their salad dressing that they affectionately have labeled "salad gravy." It is really good, and I would buy it. Roy and Kimmy also cook with a few custom-made spice mixes that are tremendous. I hope that someday they follow in A Cajun Life's footsteps and package a few of them.

*When You Go*: Given that the Retrolicious is mobile, you can't just head over to the pod and see Roy and Kimmy. However, if you are ever lucky enough to have them cross your path and bring the circus to your town, you will not be disappointed. Roy is one of the best chefs I have encountered. I particularly love their chicken and waffles, the Southern Pimento Mac and Cheese and Damn That Castro—a Cuban-style roasted pork sandwich. If Roy ever has a hamburger on the menu as a special, *get it*! With many apologies to my beloved In-N-Out, I have to admit that Roy makes the best hamburger I have ever had. If Kimmy has whipped up a batch of her red velvet cupcakes, buy them too. Don't just buy one or two; buy a dozen and take them to share with your friends and family. They are that good.

*Recipes*: You can find three Retrolicious recipes (Creamy Pimento Mac and Cheese with Garlic Kale; Damn That Castro; and Snickerdoodles) in *Trailer Food Diaries Cookbook*, Portland edition, vol. 2.

# We Just Had to Get the Food into Their Mouths: PBJ's Grilled

When Keena Tallman was in grade school in Hood River, Oregon, her grandfather Manuel would often make her carnitas with Serrano chilies. One day, he finished off this dish with local Hood River cherries, and Keena was delighted with each mouthful.

The PBJ's Grilled Food Cart has an eclectic, delicious menu that can be traced back to that warm summer day when Grandpa revealed that spicy and sweet can be combined to become something unexpected and amazing.

Now when I am at one of the PBJ's Grilled locations and I enjoy a Hot Hood—challah bread, PBJ's peanut butter, roasted jalapeño, apple wood bacon and black cherry jam—I tip my food cart hat to Keena's grandpa.

## The Oregon Country Fair

In 1993, Keena visited the Oregon Country Fair with her brother, James. James had disappeared, and when Keena found him, his hands were full with six peanut butter and jelly sandwiches that had been grilled in butter. He devoured all six and stubbornly would not share.

Keena was so fascinated by this bizarre sandwich concept that she found the vendor and got her own and absolutely loved it. It was creamy and grilled and salty and sweet. That quirky sandwich was life changing. Those two stories are the foundation of the PBJ's Grilled Food Cart.

## Grilled Peanut Butter and Jelly Sandwiches

Yep. We have a magical food cart in Portland that specializes in grilled peanut butter and jelly sandwiches. You cannot believe how good these crazy sandwiches are. My son Zayne loves the Smoking Goat—Kalamata olive bread, PBJ's almond butter, apple wood smoked bacon and apricot jam. My daughter Zoe loves the Oregonian—challah bread, Oregon hazelnut butter, Rogue Creamery blue cheese and cart-made Marion berry jam—and she always includes the duck that is an optional add-on. You read that right. Here in Portland, you can get a grilled peanut butter and jelly sandwich that comes with duck.

The Smoking Goat from PBJ's Grilled—Kalamata olive bread, PBJ's almond butter, apple wood smoked bacon and apricot jam.

## The Dream to Be Self-Employed

Business partners Keena Tallman and Shane Chapman opened PBJ's Grilled in the summer of 2010, and they have been very successful. Shane and Keena first met in Las Vegas in 2008. Both of them had wanted to be self-employed for as long they each could remember. Together, they began to conspire about opening a business.

Shortly after meeting each other, they took a short trip to Portland, Oregon, and upon returning to Vegas, Shane began researching what it would take to open a food cart in Portland. But what cuisine would they have?

Keena remembered back to that fateful day in Veneta, Oregon, at the Oregon Country Fair, and she made Shane a grilled peanut butter and jelly sandwich, telling him, "Let's do a grilled peanut butter and jelly food cart." Shane immediately said, "Absolutely not! Who would go to a food cart like that?"

The next day, Keena began to dream about making gourmet grilled peanut butter and jelly sandwiches that adults would love, and she plied Shane with the kind of sandwiches that she would make. Eventually, Shane cried uncle, and they had a cuisine for their food cart.

## From Vegas to Portland

In the fall of 2009, they sold everything, moved to Portland and began the process of finding and opening a food cart. They each got two jobs to raise additional capital. They got their first logo, planned what kind of culture they want the business to have and bought a food cart that they found in Salem. Then they found a location.

They opened on the corner of Kearney and Lovejoy. That location required them to set up and take down the cart *each* day. This went on for six months. A customer who was a huge fan one day suggested that they move to a spot that he could lease them at 23rd and Lovejoy. That spot has been home to their first food cart ever since.

## Samples Were Key

Early on, people were bewildered and confused by the concept of grilled PBJs. To solve this, Shane and Keena would go out onto the sidewalk and hand out samples. Keena was convinced that "if people would eat the sample, they would get the flavor. We just had to get the food into their mouths."

## What Would Bo Do?

In January 2011, they started to hear about this guy named Bo Kwon whose food carts empire was taking off. They decided to do whatever Bo was doing. Bo had a food cart out at Nike for lunch, and so PBJ's Grilled had to sell lunch out at Nike, too. That plan of doing what Bo was doing has paid off handsomely.

Today, PBJ's Grilled has eight to ten employees, a space at the Beaverton Farmer's Market, a busy catering enterprise and two food carts, including one at Cartopia, one of Portland's most iconic food cart pods.

*What's Next*: Keena and Shane are dreaming about having a brick-and-mortar PBJ's Grilled Café, with both cold milk and cold beer on draft, and I would not bet against them making this happen.

*When You Go*: Get two PBJ's Grilled sandwiches—a savory one and a sweet one. For savory, I love the Hot Hood or the Smoking Goat, and for sweet, I love the Joy and the Pumpkin Pie.

# Food Writer's Perspective:
## AMY BURGLEHAUS

Hi, I'm Amy, and I blog at EatingMyWayThruPortland.com. I can't promise to resolve any dining debates, but I can help you decide where you might like to go. You see, I like food. I like it a lot! I am always on the lookout for something fun and creative, and if you don't already know, Portland is booming with places that are fun and creative.

You can also follow me on Facebook as I make an effort to keep an eye on what's going on in the Portland food scene and post upcoming events. There are so many things happening in Portland all the time that it's hard to keep up, but I try. If Twitter is more to your liking, I also send out information there as well.

Portland has so much to offer, but I have to say I really enjoy the Portland food carts. Here's why: these are individuals or teams doing their own thing and doing what they love. They are passionate about food, and all they want to do is share it with you. I love that they choose something specific and really focus on it. You can find food carts that are all about cheese, crepes, pasta, Guam food, waffles, ice cream, eggs, wraps, Norwegian food, sandwiches, pork and fish—the list goes on and on. When you walk up to a cart, you never know what you might be in for. I especially love that!

I enjoy being able to talk with the food cart owners, who are also the chefs. I love hearing their stories, their struggles and their joys. When the space is small and the setting more intimate than a restaurant, you get to have that kind of a conversation with the chef. Struggles, you ask? Remember, it rains in Portland eight months out of the year. This is a tough one for these owners. Many of the pods outside of the downtown carts have really adapted well to the weather. They have covered seating, allowing you to enjoy their fare all year long.

Another thing I love about Portland food carts is that many are ecofriendly, which is very Portland, and I love it. I have been to a number of carts where my entrées have come out on real plates with real silverware. Now I'm eating for a fraction of the price on a patio with amazing food and real plates. I sometimes forget I just walked up and ordered from a window.

With all the food carts in Portland, it would be nearly impossible to hit every one of them, but it's fun trying. With all the effort I put into finding the best, I would have to say that these are a few of my favorites.

The cart at the top of my list right now is Carte Blanche. The food that they serve is outstanding. The flavor is bold, beautiful and very memorable. Aside from the amazing food, I love that these girls are in their mid-twenties, and they cook with such incredible depth—it just wows me. They change their menu often, so I can't recommend a particular dish. I just recommend you don't miss this cart.

Gaufre Gourmet is a fantastic waffle food cart. Forget about the sweet waffles with strawberries and whip cream (which are wonderful, by the way). Step out of your comfort zone and order a savory waffle. It might sound scary at first, but your taste buds will thank you. I highly suggest ordering the Spicy Goat.

Another favorite that I send many people to is the Cheese Plate. Order the Cheese Lover's Oregon Cheese Plate. You will get Oregon cheeses and cart-made crackers. The presentation is so wonderful, but I don't want to spoil it for you. Go see for yourself and be prepared to feel like you are on a perfectly planned picnic.

My family's all-time favorite breakfast food cart (yes, we even have a few of those here in Portland) is the Egg Carton. They had our attention from the moment I read about their Eggs Benedict. Yep, Eggs Benedict from a food cart, and they are perfect every time. Another item you can't miss when you visit this food cart is the FoPo Monte Cristo.

As you can see, it is easy to become passionate about the Portland food scene, especially the food carts. These vendors make my blogging a fun and easy job.

# PART III

# BREAKFAST!

## THIS COULD RUIN OUR RELATIONSHIP: THE BIG EGG

Gail and Elizabeth opened the Big Egg Food Cart on September 21, 2009, at the brand-new Mississippi Marketplace Food Cart Pod. When they met with Roger Goldingay to talk about possibly placing their cart at his pod, it was still a field. Roger took more than seventy applications for the handful of carts that first opened at Mississippi.

The Big Egg was one of the carts that made the cut. One thing is for sure: when it comes to food carts, Roger can pick the winners. Today, the Big Egg is the only food cart left from that original group. It has not only survived, it has thrived as well.

The Big Egg opened on a Monday, and it was busy from the very beginning. The first two weeks, it was word of mouth that brought lots of people to the cart. Sixteen days from its first day in business, Karen Brooks wrote an article listing the top ten food carts of 2009. The Big Egg made the cut. From the day that article came out, it has had a "sea of people" coming to the food cart.

Karen's 2009 top ten list included iconic Portland food carts like KOi Fusion, Nong's Khao Man Gai, Potato Champion and Tabor—heady company indeed. The Big Egg most definitely belongs on a list with carts like these. Not only is Karen Brooks a very talented food writer, she also knows great food cart talent when she sees it.

## Hands Down the Best Breakfast Sandwiches You Will Ever Have

I know that as Gail and Elizabeth are reading this chapter, they are both proud and slightly uncomfortable. They are very private, behind-the-scenes people. The last thing they want is the spotlight. They are also very humble. Even though it will make them cringe, I have to tell you: they can flat-out cook! There is a reason that they sell out almost every day.

## Why Breakfast?

When I asked them why they feature breakfast at their food cart, Gail and Elizabeth said, "We are obsessed with breakfast. It is our favorite meal." For years, they had wanted to open a small, intimate brick-and-mortar café together and call it the Big Egg. When they were finally ready to pull the trigger on this dream, it was 2008, and the economy was crashing. They realized that at that point a brick-and-mortar Big Egg was not possible. Then they decided to start with a food cart. (That café is still in the plans.)

## Sauces, Jams, Curds, Butters and Marmalades

One of the things that makes the food at the Big Egg so amazing is the cart-made sauces, jams, curds, butters and marmalades. Every sandwich gets one, and it adds that little extra that makes the meal extraordinary. Here is some of what I am talking about: herbed aioli made with thyme, rosemary and cayenne; balsamic aioli; lemon aioli; lemon tarragon aioli; yogurt lime sauce; roasted poblano sauce; apricot jam; tomatillo-lime marmalade; chili orange marmalade; kiwi serrano marmalade; carrot orange marmalade; quince marmalade; apricot saffron jam; sweet potato jam; chester blackberry jam; strawberry kumquat jam; nectarine jam; rhubarb orange jam; rhubarb kumquat lavender jam; rhubarb apple butter; honeyed tomato habanero butter; pumpkin butter; pear butter; orange curd; ginger lime curd; apple curd; strawberry-lemon curd; and grapefruit curd. See what I mean?

## Seven Feet by Fourteen Feet

Gail and Elizabeth are business partners and life partners. An unsung chapter in the Big Egg story is how Gail and Elizabeth have managed, maintained and nurtured their relationship through the white-water ride that is a startup. Even before the cart opened, they realized that working together ten-, twelve- and, in the beginning, sixteen-hour days in a ninety-eight-square-foot workspace could ruin their relationship.

As an entrepreneur in a relationship myself, I know how easy it can be to focus on the startup and overlook the relationship. I have seen more than one couple open a food cart and lose the relationship, and I have seen the tears of aguish that come from that path. An excellent resource for people in a relationship with someone pursuing a startup is *Startup Life: Surviving and Thriving in a Relationship with an Entrepreneur* by Amy Batchelor and Brad Feld. I can't recommend this book highly enough. The philosopher Kahlil Gibran had some wise words on the subject as well:

> *Let there be spaces in your togetherness, and let the winds of the heavens dance between you. Love one another but make not a bond of love: Let it rather be a moving sea between the shores of your souls. Fill each other's cup but drink not from one cup. Give one another of your bread but eat not from the same loaf. Sing and dance together and be joyous, but let each one of you be alone... and stand together, yet not too near together: For the pillars of the temple stand apart, and the oak tree and the cypress grow not in each other's shadow.*

When they opened their food cart, Gail and Elizabeth did not know what specific challenges their relationship would face, but they knew that rapids were ahead. When those rapids came, they worked through them as they went along. Each relationship will have different needs. Given that they are both introverts, Gail and Elizabeth learned that they each needed alone time and learned to be careful to give each other that space.

So many food carts owners and people in startups underestimate how hard it will be to keep the relationship healthy and pay the price necessary to lead a startup to success. If you are in a startup and in a relationship, I challenge you to follow the trail that Gail and Elizabeth, as well as many others, have so wisely blazed.

*What's Next*: Coming soon...the Big Egg Café. Elizabeth and Gail will make the leap to a brick-and-mortar restaurant. If they need to do a Kickstarter to help make this dream come true, I know they can count on me and many of their fans to gladly donate money. Gail and Elizabeth, I hope that you are still reading. Your fans are with you, and we believe in the beauty of your dream to open a Big Egg Café. I am also looking forward to being able to someday buy *The Big Egg Jams, Butters and Marmalades Cookbook*.

*When You Go*: Get the Arbor Lodge Sandwich. Is it breakfast sandwich perfection. Also, get whatever special they happen have. You will love it.

# STEPPING INTO A NEW LIFE: THE EGG CARTON

Tim and Sarah opened the Egg Carton Food Cart on Sunday, May 27, 2012. They had wanted to open on Saturday, May 26; however, as is common with food carts, challenges prevented that from happening.

When Sarah first started getting serious with Tim in early 2008, she told him that she wanted a new life that included a different career and a good marriage. Those are dreams that many people have. Sarah and Tim have actually pulled it off. Here is their story.

Sarah grew up in Wasilla, Alaska. She calls herself "the other Sarah from Wasilla." From a young age, Sarah loved to cook. Growing up in a small town, she had no idea that a woman could go to culinary school and pursue a culinary career. Sarah went to college in Colorado, and following college, she ended up working in retail management and corporate training. Along the way, Sarah was given the opportunity to move to the Northwest and also given a choice between Portland and Seattle. Sarah visited both cities, and Portland was the city she chose. Here is where she would put down roots.

## Are You Being Catfished?

In 2007, Sarah met Tim online playing World of Warcraft. Tim had grown up in Michigan, and when he met Sarah online, he was finishing up law school in Lansing, Michigan. In early 2008, they began chatting while playing the game, and that quickly led to e-mailing and connecting via social media.

They decided to meet face to face in April 2008. Tim flew out to Portland to meet Sarah. Both friends and family of Sarah's and of Tim's were worried that maybe they were being scammed. Tim had friends who were concerned that maybe Sarah would turn out to be a man. Sarah had friends who were worried that Tim would turn out to be a serial killer or a very bad guy.

## The Rules and the Dreams

When Sarah realized that things were getting serious with Tim, she told him her "rules" and her dreams. Sarah had had a previous relationship that left her with some pain, and she did not want to go though that again. Even before she met Tim, she told him a number of things, including her desire to someday soon change careers to an as-yet-undetermined occupation.

Sarah's ex would not taste her cooking. One of Sarah's rules was that Tim would need to have at least one bite of whatever she made. Tim was fine with all of the rules and dreams that Sarah shared with him. She was really hoping that this face-to-face meeting would go well.

Sarah and Tim Arkwright, owners of the Egg Carton Food Cart.

## Do You Want to Go Get Donuts?

Their April 2008 meeting went so well that they were married by August that same year. Early in 2008, Sarah told Tim about Voodoo Doughnuts and sent him a link to Voodoo's website. Tim noticed that people actually got married at Voodoo Doughnuts.

As Sarah and Tim were dating, the phrase, "Do you want to go get donuts?" became a euphemism for the possibility of them getting married. When the time came for a wedding, they decided to literally go get donuts. Sarah and Tim got married at Voodoo Doughnuts, and Cat Daddy officiated. Cat Daddy (whose real name is Kenneth Pogson) is one of the founders of Voodoo Doughnuts.

## Occupational Changes

Tim gradated law school and had intended to go into business law. By now, he was living in Portland with his wife, and due to the economic downturn, jobs in his field were scarce. He ended up opening his own firm. In April 2010, Sarah had just finished up her MBA but was laid off due to the recession. She received a small severance package. Tim told her that this the perfect time for her to reorganize and find another career. Sarah was thinking of maybe going into marketing or social media.

## Julia Child and Blogging

Tim and Sarah watched the movie *Julie & Julia,* and Tim very encouragingly said, "You can cook like that. Let's get you Julia Child's cookbook." In the summer of 2010, Sarah got some chickens and started a blog she called the Improbable Farmer. She began to write and cook. She focused on flavor and technique. Her newly acquired chickens began to lay a lot of eggs, and so she found herself making many egg dishes. Tim upheld his agreement and tasted every one of those dishes. He also loved them and cheered Sarah on as her culinary skills grew.

## The Best Hollandaise Sauce I Have Ever Had

The first time I ever visited the Egg Carton, I was delighted to see Eggs Benedict on the menu. I love hollandaise sauce, and Sarah's blew my mind. Early on, in December 2010, Sarah accepted a blog challenge to attempt to make hollandaise sauce for the second time in her life. The whole experience was a fiasco that included Sarah cooking in her freezer in an attempt to save her creation. Her sauce was separating, and she needed to cool it down.

Sarah ended up switching to Julia Child's recipe, making hollandaise sauce over and over again until it was perfected. When the time came to create the menu for the Egg Carton, it was Tim who strongly encouraged Sarah to put her Eggs Benedict on the menu. I am so glad that Tim did that.

## It Started with One of Tim's Signature Puns

By the beginning of 2011, Tim was ever so gently suggesting to Sarah that it would be financially helpful for her to pick a career and start earning some money. In the spring of 2011, they were driving down 82nd Avenue and passed the Cartlandia Food Cart Pod. Tim turned to Sarah and said, "Hey, you can make awesome egg dishes, and you have a lot of eggs. Why don't you start an egg food cart—you can call it the Egg Carton!"

The Egg Carton Food Cart.

One month later, they decided that they were going to open a breakfast food cart featuring egg dishes. They worked on a name for their food cart for months before finally embracing the "Egg Carton." By August 2011, they had an LLC and had purchased a food cart as well as a domain. Time to open the cart! Or was it?

## Nine Months Battling Fear

The Egg Carton did not open until May 2012 because Sarah was nervous. She was afraid of failure, and she worried about how people would receive her food. She wrestled with not being a "real" chef. A number of crippling thoughts went through her head. She did not go to culinary school—what business did she have opening a food cart? Will people even like her food?

## The First Customer

Sarah and Tim tried to open on Saturday, May 26, 2012. They had even announced on Facebook and Twitter that Saturday was going to be their first day open. I love it when I get to attend a food cart's first day. I enjoy getting to see them progress from that first day to a grand opening a month or two later and then to their one-year anniversary. I was coaching my son Zayne's baseball team, and we had a tournament game that morning that kept me from visiting the Egg Carton on their first day.

As it goes with food carts, Tim and Sarah were not able to actually open until Sunday morning. Sarah had not conquered all of her fears, and as she opened her food cart serving window for the first time, she was very anxious. Her fears came crashing down around her a few minutes later when her first customer ever showed up, and she recognized him.

Sarah calmly took the order—Eggs Benedict and three sides: a fresh fruit bowl with cantaloupe, strawberries and blueberries; rosemary potatoes; and bacon. Once her customer had gone and sat down in the tent to wait for his order, Sarah began *freaking out*. She was cursing and shaking and trying to cook. She told Tim, "#@x%. Our first customer is a #$%@!*& food writer!" She was so nervous that she burned the rosemary potatoes, and what's more, she was so shook up that she ended up serving those very same burned potatoes to her customer by mistake.

Sarah put her dishes on a tray and brought them out to the customer, who happened to be me. I fell in love with her hollandaise sauce. The burned potatoes did not even faze me. As far as I knew, it was their second day. Stuff happens when you are brand new. It was not until September 24, 2013, while interviewing Sarah and Tim for this chapter, that I found out the rest of the story and learned that I was their first customer ever.

## In Portland, Dreams Do Come True

Tim and Sarah have a successful food cart business. In July 2012, a few months after the Egg Carton opened, Tim closed down his law firm. Tim has worked side by side with Sarah in the cart since day one. "In Portland, you can just dream something up and do it!" said Sarah.

Early on in their relationship, Sarah told Tim that she wanted a new life and a new career. She was in retail management, and he was a lawyer. Now they are food cart owners and are living the life she always wanted. As she told me, "Really? People want to buy my egg dishes, and I can pay my bills doing this? How awesome is that!"

Sarah was right. In Portland, dreams do come true.

*What's Next*: Sarah hopes to write an Egg Carton cookbook. They are also planning on packaging Egg Carton Egg Spice. Someday they would like to open a brick-and-mortar Egg Carton Café specializing in breakfast and featuring Sarah's amazing egg dishes.

*When You Go*: Get the Eggs Benedict. It comes with the best hollandaise sauce you will ever have. I also really like the Famous FoPo Cristo—fried egg, chunks of bacon, Canadian bacon, cheddar cheese, spicy mustard and strawberry jam between two slices of French toast dusted with powdered sugar. Occasionally, Sarah will create a French toast special, and they are fabulous too!

*Recipes*: You can find two of the Egg Carton recipes (the Popeye with Roasted Red Pepper Aioli; and Rosemary Sweet Potato Home Fries) in *Trailer Food Diaries Cookbook*, Portland edition, vol. 2.

# The Restaurant that Opened a Food Cart: Yolk

Donald Kotler opened the Yolk Food Cart on Monday, September 5, 2011, fulfilling a long-held dream to open an establishment on Woodstock Boulevard. Donald grew up on Long Island, New York. He got his first food job at sixteen years old working at a Dunkin' Donuts in Coram, New York. Until Donald moved to Portland in 1993, New York was home base.

## *Following the Dead*

Starting in the mid-1980s, Donald began occasionally following the Grateful Dead. He would follow them for a summer tour, a fall tour or a spring tour. This allowed Donald to see the United States and the national parks, camp and travel through most of the states. Donald paid for these trips by being a rogue cook. He would set up outside the concert area and sell food to those

Donald Kotler, owner of the Toast restaurant and the Yolk Food Cart.

heading into or out of the concert. In August 1993, Donald followed the Dead to Eugene, Oregon.

When Donald told me this story, I smiled. In August 1993, my good friend Jerry Riecken took me from Olympia, Washington, to Eugene, Oregon, for my one and only Grateful Dead concert. I remember seeing those rogue cooks. Kind of funny to think that twenty years ago, Donald and I were both at that same concert. What a long, strange trip it has been.

"I came to Portland to stay for a month, and I never left," said Donald. Following the Grateful Dead concert in Eugene, Donald realized that the only states he had not yet seen were Oregon, Alaska, Washington and Montana. Donald had a friend who lived up in Portland, and he decided to stay with that friend for a month or so. Once Donald arrived in Portland, he realized that that he had finally found the place where he wanted put down roots and call home.

## A Restaurant of His Own

Fourteen years later, in 2007, Donald opened Toast. For many years, Donald had wanted to open his own restaurant. In fact, prior to opening Toast, Donald was working three jobs so that he would have the funds to move ahead with his dream when the right space became available.

Donald kept looking on Woodstock Boulevard for a place to open a restaurant. He had lived in the Woodstock neighborhood since moving to Portland, and for many years, he had dreamed of having his own place on that well-traveled thoroughfare.

In 2006, a location at 5222 SE 52nd Street, not too far from Woodstock Boulevard, became available. Donald spent nine months swinging hammers and renovating the space that for thirty years had been occupied by the Bad Ass Adult Video store. The neighborhood was very happy with the change that Donald was bringing.

"Breakfast has always been a part of me. I love breakfast. I can have breakfast for breakfast or dinner or late night. To me, egg yolk is the perfect sauce," said Donald. Indeed, from the beginning, Toast specialized in breakfast. I have eaten breakfast at Toast many times, and if you go, be sure to get a side order of griddle coffee cake. It is incredible. Before Toast, I had never had or even heard of fried coffee cake. I asked Donald about this dish, and he sat back, smiled, got a faraway look in his eye and told me a story.

When Donald was eight years old and living in New York, his grandfather would take him to a diner in Queens that sat twelve and only had counter seating. You would stand behind someone siting at the counter and wait for them to finish. Sometimes the line for one of those twelve seats was four people deep. Donald's standard order there was three pieces of bacon and a grilled corn muffin. The griddle coffee cake at Toast is an homage to those cherished diner meals Donald had with his grandfather.

## Time to Expand to Woodstock

In 2011, Donald had the resources necessary to open a food cart, and to him, that seemed like a great way to expand and grow his business. Donald had always loved food carts and food trucks, and he was excited that he was going to be able to open one himself. When Donald saw a Craigslist ad for a food cart space right on Woodstock, his heart soared. He was finally going to get to be on Woodstock.

Patrick makes the "food cart magic" happen at the Yolk Food Cart.

## Patrick Makes the Food Cart Magic Happen at the Yolk Food Cart

Most days, it is Patrick who is the person doing the cooking at Yolk. He had worked for a number of years at Toast, and it was decided that he would be the face of Yolk. When it came time to fill out the first menu for Yolk, Donald and Patrick worked together picking out the items.

## Bacon on a Caramel Roll

One of best occasional specials they have at Yolk is one of Patrick's creations: the Brioche Maple Bacon Hazelnut Caramel Rolls. Oh my, they are good! If you happen see them on the menu, get one and thank me later.

## Restaurant vs. Food Cart

Even though I love the breakfast at Yolk, there are plenty of times that I have had breakfast at Toast. Sometimes I want a food cart experience, and sometimes I want a restaurant experience. I know that some restaurateurs across the country are opposed to food carts and food trucks. They are worried that they hurt business. I consider that to be a ludicrous position. Like I said, I have cravings for both experiences equally.

Donald's opinion is that good competition can make you stronger and that the strong survive. Donald is a big food cart fan, and he loves it when a food cart is able to make the leap to brick-and-mortar.

I encourage you to visit both Donald's restaurant and his food cart.

*What's Next*: Donald has plans to open a second Yolk food cart in Portland, as well as open up a brick-and-mortar Yolk Breakfast Sandwich Restaurant. I, for one, hope that they start bottling that hot sauce. I love it, and I would buy it regularly.

*When You Go*: Two of my favorite items at Yolk involve the scrumptious pretzel bread they get from Little T American Baker. The Brother Bad Ass has maple-glazed pork belly, Beecher's cheddar cheese, an over-easy egg, greens and Dijon mustard between two slices of pretzel bread. Patrick also makes a delectable French toast from the pretzel bread that is served with maple syrup—a sweet and salty delight. Also, get a side order of potatoes just so you can put on them Patrick's signature cart-made hot sauce—roasted red peppers, honey, grape seed oil, smoked paprika and a few secret ingredients. This sauce is wonderful—spicy but not too hot and full of flavor.

# IT HAS NEVER FELT LIKE WORK: FRIED EGG I'M IN LOVE

Jace Krause and Ryan Lynch opened the Fried Egg I'm in Love Food Cart in March 2012, and one year later, they opened a second cart. Even with only two food carts, one could argue that they have the most successful food cart business in Portland. Here is their story.

Ryan Lynch grew up in Sonoma, California, and it was there that he met Jace in 2007. Jace, who then called Seattle home, had a band, and Sonoma was a regular tour stop. Jace and Ryan became fast friends who made it a point to stay in touch with each other. Along the way, even though Jace lived in Seattle and Ryan in Sonoma, they spent some time in a band together.

## Relocating to Portland and Looking for a New Career

Ryan had always had a romance with the Northwest, and in 2010, he and his wife moved here to begin a new life. Ryan had a newspaper background that started with the *Sonoma Index-Tribune*. When he arrived in Portland, he got a job with a local Portland paper and began to consider what to do next. Ryan even thought about going back to school.

Jace's professional background was working as a corporate copywriter. Jace had family here in Portland, and in 2011, he and his wife moved from Seattle to Portland. He had some money saved, and he began to look at what he could do to start a business here in Portland.

Jace began to play around with the idea of opening a food cart that served breakfast sandwiches. He eventually told Ryan about this plan, and they decided to become business partners and make it happen. Ryan left his newspaper job to work with Jace and start Fried Egg I'm in Love.

Jace Krause and Ryan Lynch, owners of the Fried Egg I'm in Love Food Cart.

## A Partnership that Started with Music

Jace had no hesitation partnering with Ryan. He knew that they would get along and be able to make it work. It did not hurt that they had played music together before. Jace shared that "working together in music is intimate, and I knew that if we could do music together, we could run a business together."

## The Name and the Weekly Specials

The name of their food cart, Fried Egg I'm in Love, is a playful riff on the 1992 Cure song "Friday I'm in Love." Every menu item and every special at the cart has a fun music theme, and Jace and Ryan have a blast thinking up new ones.

Many food carts do specials as a way of expressing creativity and avoiding becoming too bored with making the same thing day in and day out. The specials that Ryan and Jace come up with are not only cleverly named, but they are always delicious too. In my opinion, Fried Egg I'm in Love has some of the best specials of any food cart in Portland.

## *Why Breakfast Sandwiches?*

There are three reasons why Ryan and Jace choose to have breakfast sandwiches be the cuisine for their food cart. One, Jace absolutely loves eggs. Two, both Ryan and Jace love breakfast, and they fell in love with the breakfast sandwiches they were considering as they were kicking around food cart ideas. Three, and this is actually the biggest reason that they choose to feature breakfast, "from the beginning, we designed the food cart to fit our lives, not the other way around," said Jace.

They wanted to be self-employed, and they did not want their new business to own them. They wanted to be done with their workday long before 5:00 p.m. I have had scores of food cart owners tell me that during their first year in business, they worked twelve to sixteen and even eighteen hours per day for five and six and even seven days a week.

I asked Ryan and Jace a question I have asked every other food cart owner in this book: "How many hours a week did you put in, on average, your first year in business?" It took me a while to process their answer, and I even repeated the question before their response finally sunk in. "One time we worked maybe fifty or sixty hours in a week," noted Ryan and Jace.

I could not believe what I was hearing. I kept asking them about this, and they were completely sincere. They each work about forty hours a week total on their food cart business, and that has been the case from the beginning. In fact, they planned it that way; it was in the business plan they wrote before they ever opened the cart. When I told them that many food cart owners worked upward of seventy, eighty or even ninety hours per week during their first year, they were quite taken aback.

Given that that they have succeeded with their startup, grown their brand and, from the *very* beginning, worked eminently reasonable hours, one could argue that Jace and Ryan have one of the most successful food cart businesses in Portland. I tip my food cart hat to them and their business acumen.

*What's Next*: Jace and Ryan plan to get a third food cart that will be mobile and used for events and catering. I hope that someday they bottle the special seasoning they put on every one of their fried eggs. I would buy it to use at home in a heartbeat.

*When You Go*: I love the Sriracha Mix-a-Lot—fried egg, seared ham, avocado, tomato, Havarti and Sriracha on toasted sourdough. My second favorite is the Yolko Zeppelin—two fried eggs, cart-made pesto, Parmesan and two hand-pressed sausage patties on toasted sourdough bread.

# PART IV

# AN IMPORTANT PART OF THE PORTLAND FOOD CART SCENE

## SCOTT BATCHELAR: THE MAYOR OF FOOD CART TOWN

I can hear Scott right now: "Hello, Mr. Steven!" You often hear Scott even before you see him. When I hear him bellow a greeting, my heart is warmed, and I can't help but smile. I love Scott, and it is always a treat to run into him at a food cart.

In my opinion, you cannot write a book about Portland food carts without including a section on Scott Batchelar. Scott is a fixture in the Portland food cart scene. Almost every food cart owner knows him, and Scott knows about each and every food cart. Scott eats at a food cart at least five to eight times per week.

### *Scott Knows Food Carts*

Scott doesn't drive. He gets around Portland on one of his two bikes that he rides everywhere. Scott is always wearing his iconic reflective leg bands just above his ankles, and his bike helmet is never too far away.

Scott has been riding his bike around Portland, visiting food carts, since at least 2009. His knowledge about the history of Portland food carts

Scott's ever-present reflective leg bands.

encyclopedic. He can tell you with great detail who and when and where and what cuisine. He can tell you about many great food carts that have come and gone. He always knows all of the latest food cart gossip, and if you want to know about the best food carts in Portland, talk to Scott.

## Scott's Story

I have Scott's permission to tell his story, and I am very grateful to do so. Scott occupies a special place in my heart. He is incredibly intelligent, and like my eldest son, Hayden, Scott is disabled.

Scott wrote about the 2013 Portland Summer Food Cart Festival, and in that article, he said, "As some of you know I am a disabled individual." The thing is, lots of people don't know that about Scott, and truth be told, as Scott himself told me, sometimes he can be a little obnoxious.

I want to tell his story because I want you to get know him and get to enjoy the Scott that I know and love. If you run ever into him, and he is being a little bothersome or loud, you will now have a context with which to understand him.

Scott Batchelar, the "mayor of Food Cart Town."

When he and I sat down for this interview, he confessed to me that sometimes in the middle of a conversation, he will realize that he is being obnoxious, and that saddens him. During that interview, I said, "Scott, do you ever realize that you are sometimes being really loud?" His honest reply was, "I am loud sometimes?" I told him, "Yep, sometimes you are very loud." He had no idea.

If you are ever at food cart and come across a guy with a bike who is telling everyone within earshot that that particular food cart is a great one, you might have just found my friend Scott. First, listen to the man. If Scott says a food cart is worth eating at, it is. Second, go introduce yourself and invest ten or fifteen minutes listening to Scott's wonderful food cart stories.

## Belonging

It is my opinion that Scott's love of food carts is all about the community he experiences. During our interview, Scott said three things that deeply touched my heart. I heard these sentences not as a food writer but as the parent of a disabled child: "I go to the food carts for the people and the community...Food carts let me be okay with myself...Part of the reason I go to food carts is for the community, because I am accepted for who I am."

Let me close Scott's chapter with this story. He teared up when he relayed it to me while we were sitting in Teote, a Latin American restaurant specializing in street food that Scott loves. (Incidentally, Teote started out as a food cart.)

Scott's birthday is September 21, and on that day in 2011, he was asked by Bo Kwon, founder of the KOi Fusion food cart empire, to stop by the Mississippi Marketplace Food Cart Pod. (Scott loves Bo and considers him to be one of his heroes.) When Scott got to Mississippi Marketplace, Bo presented him with a cake. But not just any cake; this cake was in the shape of a bicycle. "The cake was shaped like my bike," Scott said, his voice wavering a bit.

If the Portland food cart scene were a town, Scott would be the beloved mayor.

# Roger Goldingay:
## The Mississippi Marketplace and Cartlandia Food Cart Pods

Roger and his wife, Carol, moved back to Portland in 2002. They left Malibu, California, to come to Portland. Some may shake their heads at such a choice. Those of us who know and love Portland completely understand someone choosing Portland over anywhere in California.

Roger did share with me that it was not the weather that drew him back to Portland. It was the culture we have here. "It was laid-back, less judgmental, more easygoing." He added, "Portland has a creative vibe that was very attractive...every time I read about Paris in the early 1900s, Portland came to my mind."

I said "moved back to Portland" because Roger first lived in Portland in 1975. There is an amazing little-known fact about Roger.

## Soccer

Roger was a professional soccer player in the 1970s. In 1974, the first team to ever bear the name "Seattle Sounders" took the field for the first time. They were part of the North American Soccer League (NASL). Roger Goldingay played for the Sounders that inaugural season.

In 1975, the first of four teams to bear the name Portland Timbers took the field in their inaugural North American Soccer League season. Roger Goldingay was on that team as well. He is the only person to have played for both the Sounders and the Timbers during both of their respective inaugural seasons.

Portland is known for a number of things, including the Timbers and food carts. Given Roger's love for Stumptown, it seems fitting that he would have a noted place with two of our most beloved institutions.

## Revitalizing Mississippi Avenue

When Roger came back to Portland in 2002, he moved to Mississippi Avenue, and for a number of years, he worked to buy the lot on the corner of North Mississippi Avenue and North Skidmore. By the time he was finally able to purchase it, the economy had crashed, and the lenders who were going to help him develop that piece of property were nowhere to be found.

Roger was able to get a loan from the Albina Opportunities Corporation to put in a "parking" lot with water and electrical hookups for food carts, as well as renovate the dilapidated building that was an eyesore. Roger figured that in the crashing economy, there would be a number of people who would be forced into considering self-employment, and he correctly surmised that some of those people would consider starting a food cart.

Roger's vision for that lot on the corner of North Mississippi Avenue and North Skidmore was to put in a premier food cart pod that featured some the best food carts in Portland, as well as have a great bar in the building that he was renovating.

When he was getting ready to open the Mississippi Marketplace Food Cart Pod, Roger took more than seventy applications for ten spots. Roger's goal was to pick the best carts possible. The first two food carts that Roger said yes to were Garden State (a now-defunct but legendary Portland food cart) and the Big Egg. Rogers remembered meeting Elizabeth and Gail with the Big Egg and tasting their food. He knew that they would make it.

The Mississippi Marketplace Food Cart opened in the summer of 2009, and Prost!, a neighborhood pub that specializes in German beer (or should

Roger Goldingay, founder of Cartlandia and the Mississippi Marketplace.

I say "bier"), opened in October that same year. In my opinion, Roger has done a magnificent job implementing his vision. Prost! has great beer, and it provides both outdoor and coveted indoor seating for food cart fans. The lineup of food carts at Mississippi Marketplace is consistently stellar.

Roger remembered North Mississippi Avenue before it became a highly desired Portland location. It is very gratifying to Roger to know that he has played a small role in the revitalization of that part of Portland.

## Revitalizing 82nd Avenue

With the positive changes that have occurred on North Mississippi Avenue since 2002 on his mind, Roger bought a lot on 82nd Avenue in October 2010 with the intention of putting in a food cart pod there. Right away, Roger had doubters. 82nd Avenue has/had a stigma, and people were not sure that a food cart pod could work out there.

Roger saw what others couldn't. He saw parking, bus service, the Springwater Corridor bike trail only three hundred feet away and the more than thirty-five thousand cars that drive past on 82nd every day. The

Cartlandia Food Cart Pod opened in May 2011, and it is home to about twenty-five food carts.

In the spring of 2014, Roger will be opening a pub at this pod. Like Prost!, this pub will have indoor seating and will welcome patrons to bring their food cart food in with them.


## The Landlord

While I like Roger, I would be remiss if I did not address the reality that not everyone involved in the Portland food cart scene likes him as well. Roger is a landlord, and I know firsthand that sometimes the landlord makes decisions that the tenant is not fired up about.

When we talked about what it's like to be the landlord of more than thirty food carts at a time, Roger told me that it is like herding cats. I believe him. Being a landlord to food carts is not a job that I would want.

It is my opinion that Roger feels a heavy and serious responsibility to look out for the food carts to which he rents. He loves it when one of "his" food carts succeeds, and his heart aches when one of his food carts goes out of business.


## Talk to Roger

If you are with a municipality that is thinking of implementing the Portland food cart model that we have here in the city of Portland and in Multnomah County, Roger is one of three people featured in this book that I would encourage you to talk with. Roger knows firsthand how food carts can play a pivotal role in revitalizing an urban neighborhood, and he has perspectives and wisdom that you would do well to consider.


## Portland Is Better Off Because of Roger

As a food cart fan, I am very glad that Roger had the vision to start the Mississippi Marketplace Food Cart Pod and the Cartlandia Food Cart Pod. There are a number of small business owners who would not be where they are now if it were not for Roger and his pods. If your food cart started at one of his two pods, you owe him a debt of gratitude. Portland is a healthier and more appealing city because of Roger Goldingay.

Roger, I tip my food cart hat to you, and I thank you for all that you have done for my beloved city and for the Portland food cart scene.

# Tim Hohl and Terry Travis: Friday Is Our Favorite Day of the Week

Tim Hohl and Terry Travis have introduced the people of Portland to scores of food carts though the "Food Cart Friday" segment on *First Edition*, the radio show they host on KPAM 860.

## *We've Never Had a Bad Meal*

*First Edition* launched in the spring of 2011, and by the summer of 2011, they had added a weekly food cart–centric segment. Most weeks, a food cart owner comes to the radio station and talks about their cart and brings one of their signature dishes, which Tim and Terry sample live on the air.

Tim and Terry have enjoyed more than one hundred early morning food cart meals, and they are always pleasantly pleased by how good the dishes are. Terry is very impressed that each and every dish has been wonderful.

"I live in the greatest place on Earth," said Terry Travis, who grew up in Vancouver, Washington, and graduated from Columbia River High School. Terry's career took her to places like Boston, Brooklyn and Seattle. When the chance came to come back to Portland, she jumped on it. Reflecting on that move, Terry said, "I was so glad to be coming back to Portland."

One of Terry's cherished hobbies is riding her bike. "I still remember the first time I got to ride my bike without training wheels—I felt so free!" She said that she likes to ride a long ways…slowly. One of her favorite bicycle trails is the Springwater Corridor—particularly the section that heads out toward Gresham. Out there, she encounters stunning vistas that have Mount Hood in the distance smiling down at her.

Tim Hohl was born in Michigan and lived in Detroit until his family moved to Portland when he was ten years old. He stayed in Portland through high school, graduating from Jesuit. "Portland is home," said Tim. Right out of college, Tim started in radio here in Portland. Eventually, his radio career took him north to Seattle. Thirteen years ago, the doors opened for him to come home. Portland is where his heart is. Tim really appreciates that we have both the beach and the mountains so close. He loves it that he can leave the parking lot at work and be on his skis in less than ninety minutes.

Tim's favorite hobby is beer, and he loves the Portland beer scene. "Beer is an art form," he said. His eyes danced when he told me that "in Portland you can have a different beer, every day, for 365 days, and each one will be from a local brewery and each one will be great!" Not only does he enjoy having a pint at one of Portland's many local pubs, Tim is a home brewer as well. He would love to someday open up his own local brewery.

## *I Am Out of Meatballs but I Will Fix You Up*

Tim told me this delightful story about his daughter and food carts. When Tim's daughter does not have school on Fridays, she will come into the station with him to check out "Food Cart Fridays." She was in the station the day that Jason Moreno, owner of J Mo's Sandwich Shack Food Cart, brought in the Dirty Mo. She loved it! I can't blame her, as the Dirty Mo is one of my favorite sandwiches.

It has spaghetti and cart-made meatballs on really good garlic bread. Honestly, when I first heard about the Dirty Mo, I was not really excited. Spaghetti and meatballs on a sandwich didn't sound that good to me. However, when I took my first bite, I was enraptured.

Tim Hohl and Terry Travis, hosts of KPAM 860's *First Edition*.

From that particular "Food Cart Friday" on, Tim would have to take his daughter to J Mo's so she could get a Dirty Mo. One day, something awful occurred, followed by something wonderful. Jason was out of meatballs, and consequently, the Dirty Mo could not be made. Tim's daughter was crushed. Jason, being the resourceful chef that he is, said, "Don't worry. I will fix you up!" Jason whipped up an eggplant Parmesan sandwich. Tim's daughter took one bite and *bam*—she loved it! Culinary crisis averted. That sandwich is now on the menu.

## *We Get to Celebrate a Food Cart Every Friday*

Tim and Terry look forward to the amazing food they enjoy each week during their "Food Cart Friday" segments, and they have come to love hearing the stories of the inspiring people who start food carts. As Terry told me, "Friday is our favorite day of week!"

# BRETT BURMEISTER: TELLING PEOPLE ABOUT THE COOL THINGS I FIND

Brett Burmeister is the managing editor of FoodCartsPortland.com. Brett has been writing for this website since just before the beginning of 2009. Brett has written more than six hundred food cart articles, eaten at more than five hundred food carts and dined at food carts more than one thousand times. The man knows food carts!

For the past five years, Brett has been Portland's on-the-street food cart correspondent reporting to us about all that he finds. The Portland food cart scene has grown and flourished in the city. It is my opinion that Brett is one of the people most responsible for that, and I for one am very grateful for his efforts.

Through the FoodCartsPortland.com website, Brett has made it possible for the average person to find out about food carts. He has made food carts accessible. Each time he writes about a food cart, he includes what he calls "the data"—the location, the hours, the story and a sample menu.

## Before FoodCartsPortland.com

Brett began writing back in 2005. He started a blog called "Walking in Portland," and his first post was January 19, 2005. He wrote about the cool stuff he found as he walked around Portland. In 2007, Brett was recruited to write for Portland Metblogs, which he did until June 2008.

Bret wrote a little about food carts for both of those blogs, and in the winter of 2008, he was recruited to come write for FoodCartsPortland.com. Brett had found his niche. He loves to find cool stuff and tell others about it. Going around Portland, finding food carts and then telling us about them was right up his alley.

## Tours, Consulting and Events

Not only does Brett write for FoodCartsPortland.com, he also has three other food cart–related services that he provides. He provides walking tours of food carts, during which you get small bites from four food carts, and as you traverse from cart to cart, you get the chance to hear Brett tell you about a number of very interesting food cart topics.

Brett Burmeister, managing editor of FoodCartsPortland.com.

A Big-Ass Sandwich.

The Big Egg Food Cart. *Photo by Ken Wilson.*

The Arbor Lodge Sandwich from the Big Egg Food Cart. *Photo by Ken Wilson.*

The Cheese Lovers' Oregon Cheese Plate from the Cheese Plate PDX Food Cart.

The Divine Café Food Cart.

The Killer Quesadilla from the Divine Café Food Cart.

A fried egg with Magic Egg Dust from the Fried Egg I'm in Love Food Cart.

The Grilled Cheese Grill Food Cart tagline.

*Opposite, top*: The Original Cheesus from the Grilled Cheese Grill Food Cart—two grilled cheese sandwiches, one with pickles and American cheese and a second with grilled onions and Colby jack. In between these two sandwiches are lettuce, tomato, ketchup, mustard and a ⅓-pound burger. Oh baby! Who is your big grilled cheeseburger daddy?

The school bus from the Eleventh and Alberta Grilled Cheese Grill Food Cart.

*Above*: Mac and cheese from Herbs Mac & Cheese Food Cart, topped with broccoli, bacon and tomato. *Photo by Molly Woodstock.*

*Opposite, top*: The Sampler Platter from the Homegrown Smoker Vegan BBQ Food Cart. *Photo by Ken Wilson.*

*Opposite, middle*: The Federal from the Italian Market Food Cart—Italian pork with sharp provolone and broccoli rabe.

*Opposite, bottom*: Khinkali from the Kargi Gogo Food Cart—a traditional Georgian stuffed beef and pork dumpling.

*Above*: Super Lamb Gyro from the Ramy's Lamb Shack Food Cart.

*Top*: Chicken Kabob from the Ramy's Lamb Shack Food Cart.

*Opposite, top*: A perfect latte from Olé Latte Coffee Food Cart.

*Opposite, bottom*: The PDX Six Seven One Food Cart.

Liquid Gold Thai Iced Tea from Stumptown Dumplings Food Cart, held by Nimesh Dayal.

Dumplings from Stumptown Dumplings Food Cart—Cheeky Chicken, Pompous Pork and Sassy Spinach.

The Sugar Shop Food Cart.

Strawberry cake topped with basil buttercream and balsamic drizzle from the Sugar Shop Food Cart.

The Hot Chick from the Tiffin Asha Food Cart—Pakora fried chicken drizzled with black cardamom-infused honey, pickled greens and creamy yogurt cheese wrapped in a cart-made dosa.

The Tiffin Asha Food Cart.

The Yolk Food Cart.

The Brother Bad Ass from the Yolk Food Cart—maple-glazed pork belly, Beecher's cheddar cheese, an over-easy egg, greens and Dijon mustard between two slices of Little T American Baker pretzel bread.

The Whiffies Fried Pies Food Cart.

Red velvet cupcake from the Retrolicious Food Cart.

Greek salad from Ramy's Lamb Shack—tomatoes, cucumbers and feta cheese.

The PB and J Fries from the Potato Champion Food Cart. The fries are topped with Potato Champion's peanut satay sauce and chipotle raspberry sauce.

Brett also does a little consulting. If you are thinking of starting up a Portland food cart, I encourage you to have at least one conversation with Brett. Bring a pad of paper and be prepared to take notes. If you are with one of the many municipalities that come to Portland to find out about the food cart scene, Brett is one of three people with whom you need to sit down and talk. Schedule a consultation with him and ask him to talk with you about O'Bryant Square.

Lastly, Brett works with a number of Portland's truly mobile food carts, and for a fee (paid by the food cart owner), he can help you get a genuine Portland food cart to your event!

## Brett's Favorite Food Cart

One question that Brett gets asked repeatedly is, "What is your favorite food cart?" He smiles when he tells the person that they are asking the wrong question. He goes on to say that the better question is, "Where would you take a guest from out of town?" Brett was recently asked to provide a list of the top ten food carts in Portland. He began making that list but put his pen down when he realized that the list already had forty carts and still more to go.

## Food Cart Future

I asked Brett what some of his next steps will be regarding food carts. He wants to do what he can to help further the cause of street food, and he would love tell people across the country "the glory of the pod idea." Brett has seen with his own eyes how food cart pods can improve a city and rehabilitate a neighborhood. He has a passion for food carts, and Portland is better off because he is willing to tell us about the cool stuff that he finds out there on the streets of Portland.

# RICK HUMPHREY: HIS CARD IS IN MY WALLET

Rick Humphrey is the assistant parts manager at Curtis Trailer, and if you own a Portland food cart, it is very likely that you have his card in your purse or wallet. Rick has been at Curtis Trailer since 2007, and he has been servicing food carts for many years. He has assisted many food cart owners over the years, and he has an excellent reputation among food cart owners.

## *"What Is a Food Cart?"*

Prior to 2007, Rick worked at the now-defunct Gresham RV. It was while he was working there that he first encountered a food cart owner. Rick had a customer buy a water pump. This same customer came back a few months later for a second water pump. When this same customer bought a third water pump just thirty days later, Rick's curiosity got the best of him, and he asked this gentleman what he was doing with the water pumps. Rick was told, "I use them in my food carts." Rick then asked, "What is a food cart?"

Rick had been selling water pumps to Saied Samaiel, the founder of Aybla Grill, a food cart business that today has five locations. Saied was excited to tell Rick all about the Portland food cart scene. Rick and Saied still do business together to this very day. The second food cart owner that Rick ever met was Rose Guardino, owner of the Divine Café Food Cart.

Rick Humphrey, "the Food Cart Guy."

## The Floodgates Opened

Rick did not do very much business with food cart owners while at Gresham Trailer. The owners did not really want to sell to food cart owners, preferring to stick with people who own RVs for recreational use. Once Rick moved over to Curtis Trailer in 2007, he was encouraged to go out to the food cart pods, hand out his card and help as many food cart owners as he could. Rick told me that once word got out that he was a resource food cart owners could depend on, "It was like the floodgates opened." Many food cart owners would show up to see him and get his assistance.

## A Valuable Resource for Food Cart Owners

Rick has become well versed on the health department regulations for Multnomah, Clackamas, Marion and Hood River Counties. Food cart owners regularly turn to Rick for his advice, counsel and, of course, parts! The items for which food cart owners depend on Rick include holding tanks, water pumps, water heaters, concession windows and doors, awnings, electrical cords and hasps (latches used to keep doors locked).

## Rick Humphrey, the Food Cart Guy

People began calling Rick "the Food Cart Guy," and he eventually embraced that moniker. Today, Rick has a "TheFoodCartGuy" Twitter account and Facebook page. Rick serves the Portland food cart community at a tremendous level. Many times, he has taken late-night calls to help food cart owners in need. I mentioned Rick in a conversation I was having with Jeff Mendon, owner of the Bento Box Food Cart, and he smiled and said, "I have his card in my wallet!" Every successful Portland food cart owner I know has Rick's card. Nuff said.

# BRYAN SEBOK:
# MAPPING THE MOBILE FOOD MOVEMENT

Bryan Sebok spent most of 2013 filming the feature-length documentary *Cartography: Mapping the Mobile Food Movement*, and he plans to premiere this film in late 2014.

Bryan moved to Portland in 2009 to become a professor of media studies at Lewis and Clark College. Bryan did his undergraduate studies at NC State University. He graduated NC State with a degree in mass communications and film studies. He got his masters in film studies at Emory University and has a doctorate in media studies from the University of Texas–Austin. There is a reason why Bryan is so well spoken and erudite.

Bryan also loves film. He has liked movies as long as he can remember. When he was baby, his nursery overlooked a drive-in theater, and his mother

Bryan Sebok: professor, filmmaker and food cart fan.

told of nursing him in that room while watching movies out the window. During Bryan's childhood, he got to go to the dollar theater and see a movie two to three times per week. Growing up some of his of his favorite movies were *The Goonies*, *Gremlins* and *One Flew Over the Cuckoo's Nest*.

## Visually Telling the Portland Food Cart Story

Once Bryan moved to Portland, he saw all of the food carts, and given his academic background, he did some research on them with a focus on the impact that food carts have culturally, industrially and economically. Bryan's research revealed lots of interesting data, and he found that the people who owned Portland food carts had some incredible stories. Given his love of film, Bryan began to ask himself, "Why am I not making a documentary about this amazing phenomenon?" Bryan's goal was to visually tell the story of Portland's food carts.

Bryan began filming on January 1, 2013, and he filmed at hundreds of food carts. As Bryan sat down with food carts owners and interviewed them on camera, he realized how important the story was. He observed firsthand how food carts have had positive and long-term effects on the community as a whole and on the neighborhoods in which they are located.

## Portland: A Model for Mobile Food Success

Bryan's year of research and filmmaking led him to conclude that Portland is a model for mobile food success that can be adopted by municipalities in other parts of the country. If you are with one the many municipalities that regularly visit Portland to investigate our food cart scene, I highly encourage you to sit down with Bryan and consult with him.

## Food Cart Culture vs. Food Truck Culture

Bryan has learned that one of elements that is part of the Portland mobile food success story is something that he defines as the difference between a food cart culture, where the cart generally stays in one place, and a food truck culture, where the truck is mobile and does not have a set location.

## College Students

Bryan is the kind of teacher who cares about students, and twelve of his students got to take part in the making of this documentary. I ran into Bryan a number of times throughout 2013, and I got to know two of those students: Sofia Alicastro (who served as production manager) and Alia Al-Hatlani (who worked on social media and design).

## Cheering One Another On

Over the course of the year, one of the most pleasant surprises that Bryan found was that there was less competition and more community among food cart owners than he had expected there to be. The community spirit that exists among many food cart owners touched him. Bryan himself is a food cart fan. He has many favorite food carts, including the Egg Carton, Moberi and the Smaaken Waffle Food Cart.

## Go See This Movie

I enjoy sports radio, and Colin Cowherd occasionally talks about how much he likes a good documentary. *Cartography* is going to be right up Colin's alley. It has very interesting stories, and it is set in Portland, a town that Colin knows well. When *Cartography* comes out, go see it! It is going to be a compelling, enjoyable and insightful documentary.

*What's Next*: Bryan has to get the editing completed and shepherd *Cartography* through a film festival season. Once all of that has been completed, Bryan would love to make a documentary on the craft brewing culture. Portland definitely has its share of craft breweries, too. I hope that Bryan is able to find college students willing to help make a film about beer—that could be tough.

## On Many Food Cart Menus: Carlton Farms

I was at the Burger Guild Food Cart in the spring of 2012 when Carlton Farms first came onto my radar.

### *The Burger Guild Midwest Pork Tenderloin Sandwich*

Mike at the Burger Guild makes this extraordinary Midwest pork tenderloin sandwich. The pork tenderloin is breaded, deep fried and topped with lettuce, onion, pickles and mustard. This sandwich is *huge* and incredibly good. The pork is so tender and flavorful that you want to eat another as soon as possible.

John Duyn and Jake Burns of Carlton Farms, two guys who love and know their sausage.

I noticed that on the menu, Mike was prominently featuring that he used Carlton Farms pork. As the year progressed, I saw a number of other food carts stating on their menu that they used Carlton Farms meats. Food carts were doing this to make it clear to their customers that they were using top-shelf meat from a superb local producer. It was one of the ways that a food cart could set itself apart and convey that it used first-class ingredients.

I could taste the difference, and whenever I saw that Carlton Farms was on the menu, I knew that I was in for a great meal. When it came time to write this book, I wanted to know more about this business that so many food cart owners were attaching to their brand. Given who I am, I wanted to get to know the story of this company and the stories of the people there.

## John and Jake

I was lucky enough to meet and talk extensively with two of the amazing people who make the magic happen at Carlton Farms: John Duyn, president and CEO, and Jake Burns, VP of operations. Carlton Farms was started in 1956 by Henry "Hank" Duyn. In 1958, Carl Duyn, Hank's brother, joined the company. In 1974, John Duyn was recruited to come to Carlton Farms to be the general manager. Under John's leadership, this local family business has flourished to become a very well-known and prominent local brand.

## John's Food Cart Tour

I first met John in October 2013, when I was privileged to take him on a food cart tour. We visited four food cart pods and ended up eating at seven different food carts. It was quite fun to see how excited food cart owners were to have the president of Carlton Farms at their food cart.

John earned a tremendous amount of my respect that day. He was very kind and was genuinely interested in each person we met. The encouraging way he interacted with the small business owners we met with that day was impressive.

It was apparent that John loved food and also that he was quite knowledgeable about many different types of cuisine. One minute he was conversing with Paolo from the Burrasca Food Cart about Italian food and a Tuscan butcher they both happened to know, and the next he was talking with Alec Harry from the Guero PDX Food Cart about Latin American cooking. It was also clear that John takes great pride in the fact that his company produces high-quality meats. It takes longer and costs more to do that, but for those people who want a top-shelf product, people like food cart owners, the extra investment is more than worth it.

It was John's grandfather Girard who instilled the value for making a high-quality product into the Duyn family. Girard "Jake" Duyn taught both John's father and his uncle to have an old-world charcuterie approach to meat.

"I love the science of meat and spice," said Jake Burns. It was that old-world aesthetic that caused Jake to agree to come work at Carlton Farms eleven years ago. Most large U.S. producers make bacon in about twenty-four hours. The bacon at Carlton Farms takes two to three weeks to make. When Jake learned that Carlton Farms followed the longer process, and when he saw the cure cooler, he knew that he wanted to be a part of this very special company.

Jake loves working at Carlton Farms. He graduated college with a degree in meat science, and he has loved that business ever since. If you are ever lucky enough to catch up with Jake and talk with him about meat and spice, his passion will be palpable and you know that he works for the right company.

## Two Guys Who Love Sausage

While I was interviewing both John and Jake, I asked them which Carlton Farms product was their favorite. Both of them enthusiastically proclaimed that it was sausage. Not only does Jake make sausage at work, he also makes it at home in his own kitchen. John loves sausage as well, and he is also a hot dog aficionado.

The workday starts very early at Carlton Farms. Both John and Jake shared with me that they love to grab a cold hot dog for a snack during early morning breaks. It warmed my heart to discover that John and Jake both love sausage. Why would that matter to me? That fact told me something important about Carlton Farms. Let me explain it this way: Shannon and Autumn own the Sugar Shop PDX Food Cart. This is a dessert cart, and that means that both Autumn and Shannon do a lot of baking. I mean a whole *lot* of baking, hours and hours of it. The thing is, they both absolutely love to bake, and you can tell that when you enjoy one of their amazing desserts.

The same is true when you enjoy meat from Carlton Farms. You can taste the care and the joy that goes into what it produces. I want to buy my sausage, ribs, pork, beef and bacon from a company where those in management love sausage the same way that Autumn and Shannon love to bake.

## *Truly Handcrafted*

By the way, I have been to Carlton Farms, and I was privileged to get to see behind the scenes. When they say "handcrafted," they are serious, and you can taste that difference in every bite. In my opinion, the food carts that feature Carlton Farms on their menus are making a very wise business decision.

# BRIAN WILKE AND ERIC STROMQUIST: BEING A NICE PERSON IN THE HOSPITALITY BUSINESS

I have been working with food cart owners and writing about the Portland food cart scene for two years now, and in that span of, time, I would occasionally have a food cart owner gratefully talk about a culinary school chef who trained them named Brian Wilke.

Brian Wilke and Eric Stromquist of the Oregon Culinary Institute.

I also have spoken to many chefs who have gone to culinary school, and while they always think that it is a very good idea for someone who wants to cook professionally to attend culinary school, they always say that someone should go to a "good" culinary school. They then either imply (or, more often than not, directly say) that not all culinary schools are ones you would want to attend. I decided to find out for myself who this Brian Wilke guy was and what makes for a "good" culinary school.

## *Two Nonnegotiable Conditions*

Brian Wilke and Eric Stromquist started Oregon Culinary Institute in the spring of 2006. Prior to starting OCI, they had each spent ten years working at another Portland-area culinary school. They had each started out as instructors, and before they left, Brian had become executive chef and Eric the VP of academics. Their previous culinary school ended up going though a corporate merger, and as all mergers do, this one brought a number of changes. Those changes led both Eric and Brian to part ways with that institution.

Pioneer Pacific College approached them and asked, "How would you like to start a professional culinary program for our college?" Both Brian and Eric initially said, "No thanks." Pioneer was persistent, certain that it had found the right people for the job.

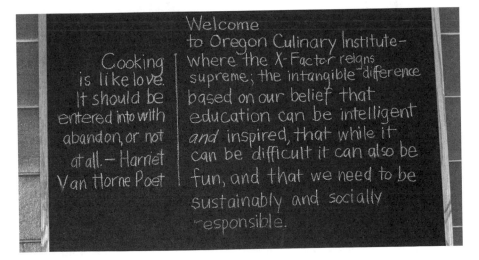

"Cooking is like love. It should be entered into with abandon or not at all," at the Oregon Culinary Institute.

Brian and Eric started having discussions with each other, and they began to remember what had first led them to fall in love with culinary education. They then said to Pioneer, "We have two nonnegotiable conditions: one, you can't tell us how to do it, and two, we keep small class sizes." Pioneer said yes to both conditions, and they began to build OCI.

Both Brian and Eric are deeply committed to small class sizes. They believe that in a hands-on environment, you need to have access to your instructor. Brian emphatically told me, "You can be in a four-hundred-person class for English. That does *not* work for cooking."

## Two Very Different Skill Sets: Cooking Great Food and Teaching Others to Cook Great Food

Eric shared with me that it took him twenty years to learn that what he liked best about the restaurant business was being a customer. His passion, as well as Eric's, is teaching others first how to make great food and then preparing them for a career in the culinary business. Brian and Eric have each worked in the restaurant business their entire adult lives, and at OCI, they were allowed to design a curriculum based on what they know their students will need out there to be successful.

## One-Third of the Incoming OCI Students Struggle with Math

Brian loves to see the students who struggle with math reach a point where they not only know that they made a really great plate of food, but that they also know how much that plate of food costs and how much they would have to sell that plate of food for to make a profit.

## You Have to Be a Nice Person

Two things really impressed me about OCI. The first was why the students do not have nametags. Brian and Eric expect the instructors to know their students' names, and that fits hand in glove with the second thing that really impressed me. If you want to be an instructor at OCI, you have to be a nice person. If during the first interview they get the sense that you are not a nice person, you won't get a second interview.

Eric and Brian see no place for the stereotypical rude and unpleasant chef in the hospitality business. As Brian said, "It's the *hospitality* business. You *have* to be a nice person." Hearing Brian say that reminded me of what John Duyn, president and CEO of Carlton Farms, said about Paolo, the owner of the Burrasca Food Cart. John said that one of the reasons why Paolo would make it as a restaurant owner (aside from his amazing food) is that Paolo has experience working the front of the house. John went on to say that he has met a number of chefs who were mean, awful people, and they can get away with that because they are hidden back in the kitchen, where the customers don't see them.

People who work the front of the house quickly learn that you need to have good people skills to keep the customers coming back. Great food alone won't do that.

## *What I Would Tell My Kids*

If one of my kids wanted to start a food cart, and they asked me what path I would suggest they take, here is what I would say. I would ask them if they wanted to simply start a food cart that would be around for a year or two, or if they wanted to start a culinary brand that would have long-term success.

If they answered the former, I would encourage them to work in restaurant for at least six months, to work in a food cart for at least six months, and then, if after doing both of those they still wanted to move ahead, I would tell them to go to a "good" culinary school like OCI.

"We teach bakers and cooks to how to make money doing what they love," said Eric. Brian added, "Our joy at OCI is equipping someone to take the passion in their heart for cooking and express it on a plate." I have no doubt that OCI is one of those "good" culinary schools that my friends who have been to culinary school encourage others to attend.

*When You Go*: They actually have a restaurant at OCI, where you can enjoy a three-course lunch or a four-course dinner made by the students. I have eaten there, and the food is wonderful.

# DOING AWAY WITH THROWAWAY: GO BOX

Laura Weiss started GO Box in July 2011 because of a conversation she had in March 2010 with a friend who worked at the City of Portland Bureau of Planning and Sustainability. GO Box is what makes it possible for you to get your downtown Portland food cart food in a reusable to-go container. As of the fall of 2013, the need for more than thirty thousand disposable containers has been eliminated because of the service that GO Box provides.

## Found Her Calling at Thirteen

Laura grew up in New Jersey, and one day when she was thirteen years old, the *New York Times* had an article about the environmental tragedy and scandal that occurred in the Love Canal neighborhood in Niagara, New York. Laura remembered feeling upset and outraged that people would have to suffer the way they did in that situation.

Love Canal—a rather large neighborhood with many homes, schools and businesses—was built on top of a site where, years earlier, twenty-one thousand tons of toxic waste had been dumped. Subsequently, many tragic health problems emerged. This environmental disaster, along with a similar situation in Times Beach, Missouri, played a major part in leading to the Comprehensive Environmental Response, Compensation and Liability Act (CERCLA), commonly referred to as "Superfund."

From that article on, saving the environment has been Laura's focus. Both her education and career have been guided by her passion to do her part to save the environment. Laura did her undergraduate work at Rutgers, getting a degree in human ecology (environmental science), a master's from UC Berkley in public health and an MBA in sustainable business from the Bainbridge Graduate Institute in Seattle, Washington.

Prior to starting GO Box, Laura worked for twenty-five years in environmental advocacy and policy, working in the corporate world for both state governments and nonprofits.

## The Conversation that Led to a Business

Laura and her aforementioned friend from the Portland Bureau of Planning and Sustainability were talking about the roughly sixty thousand disposable containers that downtown Portland food carts use each month. Most of those containers end up in a landfill. Laura herself is a big fan of food carts. She had often wished that she could take her own reusable container with her when she ate at food carts; however, health codes prevent that. At the end of that conversation, Laura's friend lamented, "If only there was a service that provided reusable containers that could be used at food carts."

That thought got Laura's mind working, and she began to think about starting her own business. She was aware of reusable containers made by G.E.T. Enterprises out of Houston, Texas, that would be perfect for food cart owners and customers. With a year, Laura had come up with an innovative business model using those very containers.

GO Box reusable to-go containers.

## The Name

Laura came up with the name for her new startup while cross-country skiing. Laura said that she does her best thinking while skiing or riding her bike. The "GO" in GO Box stands for "Green Options."

## A Community-Facilitated Endeavor

Here is how GO Box works. A person invests eighteen dollars for a one-year subscription. People can purchase subscriptions online at the GO Box website or from participating food carts. You can find a list of the participating food carts on the GO Box website as well. With your subscription, you receive a GO Box token. When you show up at a participating downtown Portland food cart, you turn in your token with your order.

Laura Weiss, owner of GO Box.

Your order is served to you in one of the GO Box–provided reusable containers. When you are finished with the meal, you take your used GO Box container to one of the drop-off sites scattered throughout downtown Portland. When you turn in your used container, you get another token that you use the next time you visit a downtown Portland food cart participating in GO Box.

In addition to the public drop-off sites listed on the GO Box website, Laura has agreements with more than twenty other corporate partners that provide drop-off sites for those people who work in that particular office or building.

Laura can be seen riding around downtown Portland on her bike dropping off clean GO Box containers to food carts and picking up the used ones so that they can be washed and made ready to be reused. Laura takes the used to containers to one of the GO Box partners who help with washing and sanitizing the used containers. Laura has two downtown restaurants and one social service organization that help with this key step in the process: the Original, Bijou Café and the Transitions Project.

## Work that Is Fulfilling and Fun

Laura loves what she does. She is making a difference for the environment, she gets to ride her bike for work, she gets to work in downtown Portland and she gets to work with food cart owners.

*What's Next*: Laura hopes to expand GO Box to other parts of the country, and she is looking at providing other entrepreneurs with licenses to use the GO Box name and concept. A city does not need food carts to be able to sustain a GO Box business. GO Box will work in any dense urban environment that has lots of office workers and lots of takeout.

# Food Writer's Perspective:
## PHIL SHEN

My fiancée, Kim Pham, and I started Behind the Food Carts (behindthefoodcarts. com) because we wanted to show the world the amazing food cart stories we were coming across. As professional photographers and videographers, we wanted to document food carts with the highest quality to match the hard work and love that goes into running a food cart.

Whenever we meet people who have visited Portland, the first thing they always mention is all the food carts they saw and ate at during their trip. Portland's food cart scene is undoubtedly one of a kind in America. The city is friendly toward food carts, and the people are friendly toward eating at food carts.

The pods conveniently placed throughout the city immediately set Portland apart. These pods allow food cart vendors to have a more permanent home than their more mobile truck cousins and let you frequent your favorite carts over and over again without having to seek them out. Food carts are an ingrained part of Portland culture. This helps push the quality forward; Portlanders are sophisticated food cart consumers. With so many amazing food carts, their expectations are high!

The food cart scene as a whole in the United States is constantly evolving. I think now that we live in the San Francisco Bay Area, we've been able to see a different side of the food cart industry and get a fresh look at our time in Portland. We definitely appreciate the focus and specialty carts that you see in Portland. Sure, there are fusion carts out there, but the Portland carts we loved most were the ones focused on doing one type of food and doing it perfectly.

A good example is Nong's Khao Man Gai. Nong and her Thai chicken over rice are a staple in the Portland food cart scene. It goes to show you what one dish done perfectly can bring to the table. It's not about having a million options to choose from that are mediocre; it's about that one perfectly comforting dish that keeps people coming back for more.

We love the opportunity that a cart can present to an aspiring entrepreneur. A new favorite of ours is Caspian Kabob. Victor saw that there wasn't enough authentic Persian cuisine in the area and wanted to fill that gap (and our stomachs) with the real deal. I grew up in the Little Persia area of Los Angeles and ate some of the best Persian food you can find in the United States, so I was extremely excited to try his cart.

Victor wasn't trying to put a radical spin on Persian cuisine or put Persian food into a burrito (which I bet someone is planning right now already). He simply wanted to bring an accurate representation of the food he is passionate about to a new audience. That's the beauty of carts in Portland. They can take a risk and introduce audiences to a whole new cuisine that they didn't even know they were missing.

We frequently get asked whether food carts are a fad. There are definitely more and more carts every year and, with that, more and more carts that go under as well. There is less room for error and more room for innovation and quality. But this is no fad; this is a lifestyle and a small business dream for a lot of chefs and owners.

It's been an inspiration to us to talk to these owners about their passion and all the hard work they put in. Sixteen-hour days seven days a week can only be summed up as a labor of love. We've been honored to be able to tell their stories and focus on not just the food but also the down-to-earth, loving people we've met along the way who share a piece of themselves with us every day through their food.

# PART V
# VEGETARIAN FOOD CARTS

## *Delicious without Meat*

## FOR THE LOVE OF CHEESE:
## THE CHEESE PLATE PDX

For more than five years every August around the time of Carina's birthday, Nick and Carina would host a gathering at Delores Park in San Francisco. The rule of this gathering was that everyone had to bring his or her favorite cheese, chocolate or sparkling beverage.

Once a year, they would spend the whole day "eating the most awesome cheese and choice sparkling wine." That event is where Nick and Carina spent many beautiful hours enjoying themselves and cherishing others. Those joy-filled days fed the amazing souls that they both are.

That annual party featuring quality cheese is the genesis of the Cheese Plate PDX Food Cart.

### *From San Francisco to Portland*

In December 2008, Nick and Carina moved to Portland, Oregon. Carina had taken the position of managing editor and publisher of *Mandala*, the official publication of the Foundation for the Preservation of the Mahayana

Carina Rumrill and Nick Dickison, owners of the Cheese Plate PDX Food Cart.

Tradition. FPMT is a very impressive charitable organization that was founded by two Tibetan Buddhist masters, Lama Thubten Yeshe and Lama Thubten Zopa Rinpoche. This organization is of the same lineage as the Dalai Lama.

## Let's Start by Opening a Food Cart

In the winter of 2012, Carina and Nick went away for the weekend to Hood River, and it was there that the idea for the Cheese Plate PDX was born. They decided that they were going start a food cart that focused on cheese. Carina and Nick spent the next few months getting ready to launch their business. For them, the food cart they were working on opening was going to be the first step in a bigger plan.

On July 6, 2012, the Dalia Lama's birthday, the Cheese Plate PDX opened its doors. The Cheese Plate PDX doesn't specialize in just any cheese. It specializes in serving high-quality local cheese. It features cheese from creameries such as Willamette Valley Cheese, Briar Rose Creamery, Portland Creamery and Rogue Creamery. If you love fine-quality cheese, the cheese plates they have will be right up your alley.

## A Vegetarian Food Cart

True confession time: I love meat. I love bacon. And I have had lots of really bad vegetarian food. In my world, hot dogs that come from a can are just wrong. The Cheese Plate, like two other food carts in this book, is a vegetarian food cart. It is serious about this vegetarian thing.

Cheese is made with something called rennet, which is, most of the time, made from the stomach of a cow, a goat or a sheep. Vegetarians are not real big on eating mammal stomachs. The Cheese Plate PDX only sells cheese that is made with rennet that is not animal based. Although the Cheese Plate is seriously vegetarian, let me be clear: I *love* the food at this cart. When I eat there, I do not miss meat. Not one bit.

Yes, the cheeses that they serve at the Cheese Plate are superb. What people tend to overlook is the amazing sides that you can get there. The menu is seasonal, so depending on the time of year, you can get items like olives, spiced nuts, truffle potato salad, roasted beets, mushroom kale pâté, cantaloupe with cardamom salt or watermelon with ginger salt.

The grilled cheese "sammiches" that they have at the Cheese Plate are a revelation. It sometimes has on the menu a lavender caramel grilled cheese sammich made with goat cheese and fontina. It is decadent. It has a seasonal grilled cheese sammich made with smoked mozzarella, roasted Brussels sprouts and caramelized onion aioli. Really? Brussels sprouts on a grilled cheese sandwich? It works. It works really well.

## Cheese for Vegans

The Cheese Plate PDX is *very* popular with vegans. I am talking real vegans—the kind who don't eat cheese. Carina said that some of her friends who are vegetarians sometimes miss meat. Vegans don't miss meat; however, some of them do miss cheese. With that in mind, Nick and Carina set out to come up with a vegan cheese that tastes good. The amazing thing to me is that they did it. They sell a cashew-based vegan fromage fort, and it actually tastes great.

"Enjoy Yourself…Cherish Others." The Cheese Plate PDX Food Cart.

## Dalai Lama Comes to Portland

For Nick and Carina, their most significant highlight to date was in May 2013, when the Dalai Lama came to Portland. The Cheese Plate PDX Food Cart and the Gonzo Falafel and Hummus Food Cart were both chosen to have their food served at a reception for the Dalai Lama. I was lucky enough to be there that day, and Carina and Nick were absolutely thrilled to be part of that event. It is funny how the universe works. In July 2012, Nick and Carina had purposely opened their food cart on the Dalai Lama's birthday, and just ten months later, their food was served at a reception for him.

Carina and Nick have a dream, and that dream is coming together. They built that dream on their love for cheese and the joy it brought into their lives back in San Francisco at Delores Park.

*What's Next*: Before 2014 ends, Carina and Nick plan to remodel their food cart and add a cheese and specialty food shop onto the end. In the long term, they would love to grow their brand to the point that they could have a brick-and-mortar establishment. I personally think that they are on to something with their cashew-based vegan fromage fort, and I will not be surprised if someday the Cheese Plate Cashew Fromage Fort is sold nationwide.

*When You Go*: First get a Cheese Lovers' Oregon Cheese Plate and whichever seasonal grilled cheese sandwich catches your eye. Then, depending on the time of the year, I have three favorites you would do well to get. If it is late fall or winter when you visit, the cheddar ale soup is on my list of the best things I have ever enjoyed at a food cart. If it is summer, and either the cantaloupe with cardamom salt or the watermelon with ginger salt is available, get it!

*Recipes*: You can find three of the Cheese Plate PDX recipes (Cilantro and Goat Cheese Spring Rolls with Peach Chutney; Wild Mushroom and Kale Pâté; and Fromage Fort) in *Trailer Food Diaries Cookbook*, Portland edition, vol. 1. Two more of the Cheese Plate PDX recipes (Smoky Caramel Grilled Cheese; and Spicy Kale and Garlic Cheese on Toast) can be found in *Trailer Food Diaries Cookbook*, Portland edition, vol. 2.

# I Hitchhiked My Way to Portland: Divine Café

Some food cart owners will say, "Back when I opened my cart, the Portland food cart scene was just getting started." In the fall of 2013, I was privileged to attend the twelfth anniversary of the Divine Café Food Cart. That's right, I said twelfth. The Divine Café Food Cart has been around for twelve years. When the Divine Café Food Cart moved to the 9th and Alder pod, it was the fourth food cart to open there.

One of the tough parts of being a food cart fan is seeing how many of them go out of business. Often a food cart owner's initial goal is make it through the first winter, and it is quite an achievement for a food cart to make it through two winters. The Divine Café has been through thirteen winters.

Rose Guardino visited Portland in the summer of 1990, and in 1991, she graduated high school, having attending Santa Catalina School for Girls in Monterey, California. Following graduation, Rose knew that she wanted to live in Portland, and she proceeded to hitchhike her way to the "City of Roses" itself. She then spent nine years working in the restaurant business. During that time, she worked in both the front and back of the house and attended culinary school. Rose had been professionally cooking for a number of years before attending culinary school, which taught Rose to think in ounces and pennies and helped her realize how important each of those pennies and ounces were to succeeding as a small business owner working in the food industry.

## I Want to Open a Food Cart

Rose opened the Divine Café Food Cart in 2001. In March 2000, she was going through a tough transition phase in her life, and a friend asked, "What do you want to do with your life?" Rose answered, "You know that Snow White Food Cart downtown? I want to open a food cart, a vegetarian food cart."

In May 2000, while meditating, Rose saw the name that her food cart would have—the concept, the colors and so on. Rose then began putting together a business plan. At this point in her journey, Rose also worked with a SCORE mentor, and she found that experience to be extremely helpful. SCORE is a nonprofit association that provides entrepreneurs access to coaching from active and retired businesspeople who have had success in

Rose Guardino, owner
of the Divine Café
Food Cart.

their field. The company was previously known as the Service Corps of
Retired Executives, but it is now recognized as SCORE, "Counselors to
America's Small Business."

## Every One of Us

Rose occasionally gets asked, "What does the name of your food cart mean
to you? Are you trying to make a religious statement?" Rose believes that
none of us is perfect and that each of us is divine and special. Rose wants
people to know that that they are worth it. She loves providing people with
healthy, high-quality food that is delicious, and she hopes that her food helps
people realize that good food can also be healthy.

## Leaving 9th and Alder

In 2006, Rose was given the opportunity to open a food cart on the campus of the National College of Natural Medicine located near the Ross Island Bridge just off of Southwest Naito Parkway. She bought a second food cart and, for a time, had two carts opened. Rose ended up selling her first food cart, which was located at 9th and Alder, to Kir Jensen, who opened the Sugar Cube Food Cart in that very cart.

The Divine Café Food Cart remained at the National College of Natural Medicine until July 2012, when Rose moved to the Good Food Here Food Cart Pod on 43rd and Belmont. Rose has done very well at her latest location. The Divine Café Food Cart now has a beer and wine garden, and Rose was among the very first food cart owners to get an Oregon Liquor Control Commission (OLCC) liquor license for a food cart.

## Grimm

A number of Portland food carts have a connection to the TV show *Grimm*. Rose actually works on the show, serving as a food stylist. She really enjoys seeing food that she has styled end up on TV.

## A Vegetation Paradise and Great Food for the Rest of Us

As I have mentioned elsewhere in this book, I love bacon, and there is nothing like the smell of meat cooking over a flame. That being said, when I eat at the Divine Café, I thoroughly enjoy my meal. In fact, only about 25 percent of Rose's clients are vegetarians. The majority of her customers are people who simply go for the wonderful food.

*What's Next*: Rose plans to expand the catering that she does out of her food cart, and she hopes to continue to do even more food styling for the TV and film industry.

*When You Go*: Get the quesadilla! It is delightful. The Tempeh Rueben is stellar, as is whatever soup and dessert they happen to be serving that day. I think that I could live on the wonderful soups they have at the Divine Café.

# PEDALING KALE: MOBERI

*I'm Ryan with Moberi, and we make smoothies with bikes!*
*—Ryan Carpenter from the 2013 Moberi Kickstarter*

Ryan opened the Moberi Food Cart in August 2012, launching one of Portland's most innovative food carts. At Moberi, they ride a bike hooked up to a blender to make phenomenal smoothies that taste fantastic and are quite healthy for you.

"None of the traditional options appealed to me," said Ryan. When he was in high school, he would hear about career options that he could pursue following college. It was then that he realized that he would most likely end up being self-employed. Working "nine to five" Monday through Friday for the "man" for forty years was not a path that Ryan wanted to take.

In his twenties, Ryan traveled the world. He would say that he was looking for the perfect business idea. Ryan always said this half jokingly and with a smile…but only half jokingly. Someday he would have to start his business; he just did not know what it would be.

Ryan Carpenter, owner of the Moberi Food Cart.

Ryan traveled the globe, seeing South America, Europe, Vietnam, Australia, New Zealand and many other places. Ryan had a number of adventures along the way, and I hope that someday he writes about them. For example, in Morocco, Ryan met a very special turtle named Mo and even ran out of money and ended up sleeping on a roof for a few weeks.

## Inspiration Struck in the Land Down Under

Ryan is not a trust fund baby, and he funded much of his traveling working odd jobs as he roamed the planet. In Australia, he had part-time job washing dishes, and a coworker showed him a YouTube video featuring a Guatemalan NGO named Maya Pedal. Maya Pedal makes a number of bike-powered machines. Ryan knew then that he had found the business idea that he had been searching the world over for.

## It Started on the Sidewalk

In 2010, he returned home to Portland, got a job to pay the bills, bought a journal and began to sketch out his new business. In the spring of 2011, Ryan set up a bike-powered blender on the sidewalk in front of his house. He had a modified Schwinn, a blender, a cooler full of fruit and a dream. People liked his smoothies, and over that summer, he hauled around the bike, the blender and a portable sink and made smoothies at events all over Portland. Moberi was on its way!

## The Name

Moberi is so named to honor Ryan's turtle Mo, as well as because Ryan likes the awesome berries that we have in Oregon. One day, that name popped into his head, and once he said it out loud, it stuck. He knew that he could build a great brand around that name.

"Money aside, Kickstarter was the best thing I ever did for my business," Ryan noted. He bought his first cart in 2012 and opened up at a food cart pod in August that same year. He soon realized that he would do well to have a second food cart that he could use for events, and on April 12, 2013, he launched a Kickstarter project. Ryan was able to raise the $6,000 he needed

The Delorean from Moberi.

for his second cart. In addition to the needed funds, he also got two huge unexpected benefits from his Kickstarter efforts.

The first was that in preparing for his Kickstarter, he basically had to sit down and finally write a comprehensive business plan. He found that process to be immensely valuable. It is actually common for food cart owners to open their food cart without a business plan.

The second unexpected benefit was the Kickstarter video itself. That video allowed people to see what Ryan means when he says, "Moberi is smoothies powered by bikes." I tell food cart owners all the time that you have to tell people your brand story, and the Moberi Kickstarter video does just that for Ryan. Go watch the video for yourself and see what I mean. Ryan is very grateful to Ken Wilson for the work he did filming and editing that video.

## Pedaling Kale

Ryan has done a fantastic job providing amazing smoothies that taste great and have ingredients like kale, beets and spinach in them. I have to admit, the first time I had one of Ryan's healthier-sounding smoothies I had some fear and trepidation. But wow, Ryan's concoctions are great—even the ones with kale!

Ryan's two most popular smoothies are the Delorean (strawberries, banana and mango) and the Captain Planet (kale, spinach, mango, banana, hemp protein, ginger and coconut milk). In addition to those smoothies, you can get an Uncle Jessie, a One Night in Bangkok, a Johnny Utah and others.

The next time you are in Portland and want a smoothie, go to Moberi!

*What's Next*: Ryan is working on a smoothie cookbook, and then he hopes to launch a website where he will share some of his travel stories and talk about the lessons he has learned on his startup adventure.

*When You Go*: My favorite Moberi smoothie is the One Night in Bangkok, a savory smoothie made with peanut butter, Sriracha, sesame oil, banana, whey protein and almond milk. For me, it is the crème de la crème of the smoothie world. Whenever I have one, I feel smart enough to play chess.

*Recipes*: You can find two Moberi recipes (the Delorean; and Turtle Power) in *Trailer Food Diaries Cookbook*, Portland edition, vol. 2.

# WHOLE HAWG VEGAN: HOMEGROWN SMOKER VEGAN BBQ

Jeff Ridabock opened the Homegrown Smoker Vegan BBQ Food Cart in April 2009. He himself became a fully fledged vegan two months later.

## *The Economy Was Crashing and the Kids Had Become Vegan*

For many years, Jeff worked at a corporate job that he loved. He was a chef consultant in the food services industries. In 2008, he lost his job, and as he looked toward finding new employment, he discovered that the only jobs he could get in that industry were going to pay him half or even less than the one he lost.

In 2006, Jeff's two teenage kids came home one day and announced that they were now vegetarian. Jeff, being a chef in his own right and the one who did all the cooking in the house, started learning to cook vegetarian. Two years later, his kids decided to go vegan, and Jeff was faced with learning to cook without butter, cream or cheese.

This culinary challenge actually invigorated him. Jeff found that he loved getting to be creative in the kitchen once again. The more he cooked vegan cuisine, the more excited he got. He found that he could make vegan food that tasted great.

Jeff had previously been involved with a Westside company that did meat barbecue. The more he cooked vegan, the more the idea of applying barbecue techniques to vegan cuisine appealed to him.

## Perhaps a Food Cart Is the Next Step

In late 2008, Jeff began to realize that instead of taking another corporate job, he could choose the self-employment route and open a food cart. Jeff then began to toy with the idea of opening a vegan food cart. His big question was: would people buy his vegan concepts and dishes?

In early 2009, Jeff did the cooking for his son's birthday party, and all the items were vegan dishes prepared with barbecue techniques. He wanted to see if young people would like his food. The items were a huge hit, and by the time that party was over, Jeff knew that he could make a vegan barbecue food cart work.

## What to Name the Food Cart?

Jeff had the master bathroom mirror peppered with post-its that had potential names on them. Yet he did not like any of the names that he came up with. It eventually came down to three concepts. Jeff felt that this was homegrown business, the food was vegan and much of it was prepared with barbecue techniques. Eventually, he settled on calling his cart Homegrown Smoker Vegan BBQ. To Jeff, this name was memorable, fun and accurate.

## *Vegan and BBQ?*

I asked Jeff, "How can your cart be vegan *and* barbecue?" Jeff's answer made sense to me. He uses natural woods and smoke, and he cooks at a low temperature. He uses rubs and marinades and sauces. Jeff employs the same techniques now that he used when he was barbecuing meat.

Jeff Ridabock, owner of the Homegrown Smoker Vegan BBQ Food Cart. *Photo by Ken Wilson.*

## The Ups and Downs of Running a Food Cart

Jeff first opened his cart on 23<sup>rd</sup> and Alberta in 2009. By the time 2012 rolled around, Jeff had two food carts—one downtown and one at the now-defunct Green Castle Food Cart Pod. Jeff was able to make two carts work for nine months before he had to shut down one of his carts and move the other. The year 2012 was a rough one, and Homegrown Smoker Vegan BBQ almost did not make it.

Thankfully, Jeff was able to move his remaining cart to the Mississippi Marketplace Food Cart Pod, and the summer of 2013 was his best ever. The future of Homegrown Smoker Vegan BBQ is once again looking bright.

## The Cream in the Coffee

Jeff actually had a tough time himself going vegan. Just before his cart opened in 2009, he had given up the last bit of chicken and cheese that he had occasionally nibbled on. With all the vegan dishes that the had learned to cook, giving those two items up was no big deal. The cart had been open two months, and Jeff was still having two ounces of cream in his coffee each morning. It was then that he told himself, "Jeff, if you are going to go vegan, you have to go whole hog [or "hawg," as he often puts it]." With that, he became 100 percent vegan.

Jeff is quite a character. He is often wearing a tie-dyed T-shirt, and he calls himself a "psychedelic relic." And yes, I did ask—the Grateful Dead is indeed his favorite band. Jeff and his vegan food cart are very much a part of the always interesting Portland food cart scene, and he has many vegan fans who count on him for their supply of vegan 'cue.

*What's Next*: Jeff has been working on a cookbook, and he gets many requests to bottle and sell his barbecue sauce.

*When You Go*: Get the Slosmomofo—smoked soy curls with a maple bourbon barbecue sauce and a chipotle slaw. I also recommend the smoked tempeh burger. If you want to sample a number of Jeff's dishes, the combo platter is the way to go.

# Food Writer's Perspective:
## JENNIFER CHAN

Portland is a city of many things, but from my visits, I see a city of determined and innovative people. It is a city of intense lovers, so focused in the "what" yet cognizant of the need for the social glue to make it also about the community they're raising around it.

Portland's food cart scene is nearly legendary, and yet I still had no idea how robust it was. Nor did I realize how intimidating it would be to even begin. Ultimately, I started with the Frying Scotsman. I couldn't have picked a better cart—James King is such a character and so willing to share his story. Eventually, I would pick out the craziest carts or the ones with dishes I'd not seen. Those are the carts with a story behind them—they're doing something out of the ordinary either with their décor or in their kitchen.

The maturity in Portland's food cart scene is the thing that I wish for most in other cities. Seeing how pods have fostered a real community space was also really eye-opening. Food trucks in other cities don't have the advantage of a permanent area to stay in, and so they never have the chance to establish something more than transient with the people they serve. I can only hope that other cites embrace the unique Portland pod concept—it's a great way to create real ties beyond service.

In the end, great food carts are not just about a good product; they are about the people behind it. There are plenty of carts out there that are there only to feed your hunger, but the ones that stand out are the ones that share their enthusiasm and connect with you. Whether by verbal means or beyond by using social media, it's the connection that will keep people coming back. Social media plays heavily into that these days, but it's more because that is where a large portion of their audience lives. Sometimes just talking face to face is the best way.

For those visiting and wanting to get right into food carts, I'd tell them to do some research first. Having an idea of what's worth eating will cut down on all the aimless wandering. Here are my top food cart dishes:

Khachapuri from Kargi Gogo. This hot bread oozing with cheese and with a lightly crisped exterior is the perfect carb-bomb. With salty melted butter running down my chin, this just hit me in all the right ways right from the first bite.

Liège Waffle from Gaufre Gourmet. It's the smell that gets you first—that distinctive smell of caramelizing sugar and yeast. But what spurs you on is the waffle's crunch from sugar and an extra toasty exterior. Then there's the "just right" give of a perfectly chewy interior. I love these over Belgians as the liège-style waffle gives your teeth something to sink into.

Fish and Chips from the Frying Scotsman. This classic dish is just done really well here. The batter is airy and not greasy, the fish is perfectly done and the fries are amazing. Love that hint of turmeric in the batter.

Carnitas al Güero from Guero. I've had little experience with Mexican sandwiches, but these were just flat-out delicious. Great punchy flavors, but they are still really well balanced, encased in these fluffy breads with just the right give. So good.

Eggs Benedict from the Egg Carton. Love their take on the classic eggs benny. Tangy lemon hollandaise sauce over beautifully poached eggs and a cart-made sausage patty. Then topped with a hit of saltiness from the kale chip.

Kelaguen Mannok from PDX Six Seven One. Cold and smoky chicken cubes liberally mixed with coconut, peppers, onions, lemon and a good kick of chili. Ridiculously good. My mouth is watering as I type this.

Arbor Lodge Sandwich from the Big Egg. A perfect breakfast sandwich—meaty, but not in a way that would weigh you down. The garlicky goodness and peppery bite of arugula are perfect touches. And of course, it's finished with a fried egg. Terrific.

# PART VI
# CUISINE FROM AROUND THE WORLD

## EAT SOMETHING GEORGIAN (AND WE ARE NOT TALKING PEACHES): KARGI GOGO

McKinze Cook and Sean Fredericks opened the Kargi Gogo Food Cart on March 20, 2013. Their path to 9th and Alder took them from Iowa to Akhaltsikhe, Georgia, to Portland.

### *We Wanted to See the World*

Both Sean and McKinze attended the University of Iowa in Iowa City, Iowa—Sean for his graduate degree (an MBA) and McKinze for her undergraduate degree (in anthropology). When they met in 2006 in Iowa City, McKinze was working for the chamber of commerce, and Sean was the manager of the Englert Theater, a nonprofit performing arts venue.

McKinze and Sean became a couple in 2007, and they were married in 2009. Both of them wanted to see the world, and they applied to the Peace Corps. They were accepted and were notified that they were going to spend two years serving in the country of Georgia. They left the United States in April 2010 for an amazing adventure.

When they landed in Tbilisi, they knew how to count to ten in Georgian, and they could say, "I am not hungry" and ask, "Where is the bathroom?" Sean and McKinze spent three months in language training in Kvibisi, a small village outside Borjomi, home of Borjomi Mineral Water. It was there in Kvibisi that they fell in love with khachapuri, one of the best things that you will ever eat.

## Making a Difference and Enjoying Great Food

Once their training was complete, Sean and McKinze moved to Akhaltsikhe, where they lived with a host family until July 2012. Both of them worked with nongovernmental organizations/nonprofits in Georgia, helping them (the NGOs) to become more effective and efficient. McKinze worked with organizations that dealt with women's health issues, and Sean worked with a few NGOs, including a youth center that taught teenagers leadership and computer skills.

One of the ways that McKinze and Sean connected with their host family was learning to cook Georgian dishes. Inga, their host "mom," taught them to make the dough for khinkali. Sean and McKinze also became friends with Nino and Dato, who owned the Saghighino restaurant. It was in the kitchen of Saghighino that Sean and McKinze learned to fold khinkali. Making this amazing food in Georgian kitchens is the reason why Sean and McKinze can prepare authentic Georgian cuisine today. Little did they know how these skills would serve them later.

Feasting is a huge part of Georgian lifestyle, and this makes perfect sense when you discover that Georgia is the birthplace of wine and home of the oldest wine-producing regions in the world. Sean told me that wine is an integral part of Georgian culture. Almost every weekend, Sean and McKinze got to enjoy a traditional Georgian supra (feast).

## Vacation in Portland, May 2011

In May 2011, Sean and McKinze took a vacation back to the United States, and they came to Portland. They were trying to decide where they might move to once their service in Georgia was over. It was down to Chicago and Portland. While here in Portland, they even went to the 9th and Alder food cart pod and had a meal. By the summer of 2011, they had decided to move

Khachapuri from Kargi Gogo, the best cheese bread that you will ever have.

to Portland. Now they just needed to figure out what to do for income once they got here.

## The Culinary Beauty that Is Khachapuri

Khachapuri is Georgian cheese bread. When you get khachapuri, the cheese is between two pieces of fried bread, and it is melted and warm and ready for you to devour. Khachapuri is a salty, cheesy delight. Some people say that it is the best cheese bread in the world. It is certainly one of the best things that I have ever eaten. There is only one way that khachapuri could get even better.

## A Stack of Khachapuri Gave Them Their First Answer

On a fall Saturday morning in 2011, McKinze and Sean were in their bedroom talking about what they could do for income once they moved to Portland in 2012. Sean had always wanted to open a restaurant or do something with food, and this long-held dream was a part of the conversation.

Inga, their host mom, called them down for breakfast. As was usual for a Saturday morning, there was stack of khachapuri. As soon as McKinze saw the steam rising from the stack and the melted cheese oozing from the sides, she turned to Sean and said, "We need to do Georgian cuisine!" Within two months, they had decided that when they got to Portland, they would open a food cart serving their favorite Georgian dishes. Now they just needed a name for their food cart.

## Tony Gave Them Their Second Answer

In May 2012, some of their friends from Iowa came to Georgia and stopped and visited with Sean and McKinze. A very common expression in Georgia is "kargi gogo," which means "good girl." Upon hearing the explanation for this phrase, Tony said, "That would be a good name for your food cart." Tony is also the person who later designed the Kargi Gogo logo.

## Six Months to Open a Food Cart

Sean and McKinze arrived in Portland on September 25, 2012, and they began making preparations to open their food cart. They both got jobs in the restaurant industry, Sean as a line cook and McKinze as a hostess. They did this to learn just a little more before opening their food cart. In February 2013, they found a food cart that was available right at the same 9th and Alder food cart pod where they had eaten just twenty-two months earlier.

## Ambassadors of Georgian Cuisine

Even before they opened Kargi Gogo on March 20, 2013, Sean and McKinze received support from Georgia. Georgians are fiercely proud of their culture and cuisine, and they were very honored that Sean and McKinze were promoting both here in America. I am delighted that Sean and McKinze chose Portland over Chicago, and I look forward to seeing how they grow their fledgling startup.

*What's Next*: Sean and McKinze have big plans for the Kargi Gogo brand. I myself am hoping to one day be able to go into a brick-and-mortar Kargi

McKinze Cook and Sean Fredericks, owners of the Kargi Gogo Food Cart.

Gogo and have a cold beer with a plate of warm khachapuri. In my opinion, the only way to improve on the melty, cheesy goodness that is khachapuri would be to enjoy it with a cold beer and a playoff football game.

*When You Go*: Need I say it? Get some khachapuri! I also love the khinkali (a stuffed beef and pork dumpling) and the badrijani (a vegan dish that has a puree of walnuts, garlic and Georgian spices wrapped in strips of sautéed eggplant).

*Recipes*: You can find the Kargi Gogo recipe for Khinkali in *Trailer Food Diaries Cookbook*, Portland edition, vol. 2.

# SO MUCH MORE THAN JUST CURRY: TIFFIN ASHA

Elizabeth Golay opened the Tiffin Asha Food Cart on May 17, 2013. Since then, it has received quite a bit of well-deserved attention, including being named one of the top-ten new food carts of 2013 by Michel Russell, the restaurant critic for the *Oregonian*, as well as being featured in a very complimentary August 2013 *Portland Monthly* story written by Karen Brooks.

## *Inspired by a Cookbook and a Restaurant*

Elizabeth met her future wife, Sheila, in 2002 in Seattle, Washington. In 2004, they began dating, and in 2006, they moved to Boston. While there, they were married in Cambridge. Sheila's family is from South India, and back when they were dating, Sheila loaned Elizabeth her copy of *Dakshin*, a cookbook written by Chandra Padmanabhan.

Elizabeth Golay, owner of the Tiffin Asha Food Cart, and her wife, Sheila.

*Dakshin* features cuisine from South India, and Elizabeth quickly fell in love with the food from this part of the globe. Sheila and Elizabeth lived in Boston from 2006 to 2009. During this time, Elizabeth, a culinary school–trained chef, worked at Oleana for the James Beard Award–winning chef Ana Sortun. Elizabeth was able to get a front-row view to what a chef could do with a cuisine he or she loved. It was then that Elizabeth began to dream about what she could do with the cuisine of South India.

Elizabeth noted, "I was sick of working hard for someone else and not getting anything for me. I wanted to work hard for myself, building my own business." In 2009, Elizabeth and Sheila moved back to Seattle, and Elizabeth went to work as a pastry chef at Poppy, a much-acclaimed restaurant on Capitol Hill started by Jerry Traunfeld, the James Beard Award–winning chef who worked as the executive chef at Herbfarm from 1990 to 2007.

By late 2010, Elizabeth had decided that she was going to open her own restaurant and that she was going to begin this endeavor by starting a Seattle food truck. Before she could pull the trigger on this decision, Sheila came home one day and said, "How would you like to move to Portland?" Sheila had been offered a job in Bridgetown.

## Falling in Love with Portland

Sheila and Elizabeth moved to Portland in January 2012, and they loved what they found here. "The people are wonderful, it is small business oriented and it is a place where you can be yourself," said Elizabeth. Even before they arrived in Portland, it was decided that Elizabeth would open a food cart here. Seattle's loss became our gain.

For the next year, Elizabeth's "job" was perfecting the items that she would put on her menu. Sometimes a food cart can be opened a few weeks or even a few months before the owner has nailed down the cooking side of their business. I first ate at Tiffin Asha on May 17, 2013, and from the first day that they were open, the food has been incredible. Elizabeth is a *very* talented chef.

## Dosa Is the Canvas

When you go to Tiffin Asha, you will find a number dishes with which you may not be familiar: dosa, sambar, vada and so on. Dosa is a paper-thin fermented rice and dal (lentil) crepe. Start out with the Hot Chick—most everybody does. The Hot Chick is a pakora fried chicken drizzled with black cardamom-infused honey, pickled greens and creamy yogurt cheese wrapped in dosa.

Sambar is a delightful soup that reminds me of a tomato soup for grown-ups. Get some idli and dip it in your sambar. Vada is a savory donut, and the vada at Tiffin Asha are made with coconut-chili fleur de sel. They are scrumptious.

### *You Can Get Very Creative: Chutney and Gunpowder*

Two of the fun things about eating at Tiffin Asha are the chutneys and the gunpowder. You can get one of four cart-made chutneys that allow you to change the flavor profile of each bite simply by switching from one chutney to another. I love to spread the coconut chutney on my vada.

You can also get three different flavors of "gunpowder," which is Elizabeth's take on podi. Podi is a mix of dry spices that you combine with sesame oil just before you enjoy it. At Tiffin Asha, you are given a packet of

Chef Elizabeth Golay making dosa at the Tiffin Asha Food Cart.

gunpowder and a little cup that has sesame oil in it. You empty your spice packet into the little cup and voilà! You have yet another flavor with which you can experiment.

Between the four chutneys and the three gunpowders, you have seven extra ways to personalize and season your food. Make sure that you get extra dosa and vada to enjoy with your combinations. Have fun with it. Remember when you were a young child, and you got to finger-paint and would fearlessly swirl different colors together to see what would happen? You can do the same with your chutney and gunpowder.

## The Art of Making Dosa

Elizabeth had come up with her own recipe for dosa that she spent a year perfecting. She combines two kinds of rice (basmati and sona masoori) and three different kinds of lentils (chana dal, urad dal and fenugreek seed) and soaks that mixture overnight in a big container. Over night, it rises and ferments.

In the morning, Elizabeth whisks up this mixture and puts it in the fridge to chill for a few hours. When it is time to make dosa, the chilled liquid is poured very thinly onto the hot grill. Watching Elizabeth make dosa is quite mesmerizing, and you can tell that you are seeing an artist at work.

## Bringing the Cuisine of South India to Portland

Elizabeth loves it when people who are not familiar with food that she specializes in come to her cart, learn about it and enjoy it. She told me that when many people in the United States think of Indian food, they think of curry, and she relishes helping people discover that there is much more than just curry to embrace when it comes to this cuisine.

I have to say that I think it is time for a Portland food cart chef to win a James Beard Award, and I think that Elizabeth Golay is a worthy candidate.

By the way, "Tiffin" means "snack," and "Asha" means "hope" or "wish." It is my hope that Elizabeth will be able to see her food cart dreams come true.

*What's Next*: From the very beginning, the plan was to build the Tiffin Asha brand to the point that a small, intimate brick-and-mortar Tiffin Asha was feasible. I hope along the way that Elizabeth packages her gunpowder and chutneys. I would buy them to use at home in an instant.

*When You Go*: Take a friend with you, order three or four dishes, get some gunpowder and some chutney and have a blast enjoying amazing food the likes of which you may have never had before.

*Recipes*: You can find the Tiffin Asha recipe for Coconut Chutney in *Trailer Food Diaries Cookbook*, Portland edition, vol. 2.

## BECAUSE OF MEATBALLS AND GRANDMA CLENORA: VIKING SOUL FOOD

Megan Walhood and Jeremy Daniels opened Viking Soul Food on August 19, 2010. When a food cart first opens, the owner is hoping to be able to make it through the first winter. Viking Soul Food has made it through four winters and shows no signs of stopping.

Viking Soul Food features Norwegian cuisine, and the menu is primarily built around the Norwegian flat bread know as lefse. This food cart has received quite a bit of press. It was in a *Food and Wine* magazine feature on

Megan Walhood and Jeremy Daniels, owners of the Viking Soul Food Cart.

Nordic food, and in 2012, the *Smithsonian* magazine named it one of the twenty best food carts in the United States.

## Where All Good Love Stories Start

The Viking Soul Food story started where many good love stories have started: the kitchen. In 2006, Jeremy and Megan met in the kitchen at Nostrana, one of Portland's best restaurants. By 2007, they were a couple. "I am a chef, and I figured out that I was not really good at working for someone else and that I was not good at middle management. They left me needing to start my own business," said Megan, who grew up in Portland.

## To the Antarctic and Back

Following high school, she began to see the world, cooking along the way. The first stop was Olympia, Washington, to attend Evergreen State College. "Greeners" (as the locals refer to the students at Evergreen) are a special bunch.

One common Evergreen joke suggests that "patchouli oil is considered an aphrodisiac at Evergreen." Archibald Sisters is a local Olympia business that sells many different fragrances, including peach, sandalwood, wisteria and blackberry. There is a reason why two of the fragrances you can get at Archibald Sisters are patchouli and patchouli vanilla.

Following her time at Evergreen, Megan began cooking. Her first stop was a restaurant cherished by locals and now gone: Olympia Restaurant, also known as Ben Moore's. In 1999, Megan went to Antarctica to cook and hang out during the approaching Y2K crisis. The world did not end, and Megan headed off to New Zealand for three years. Finally, it was time to come home to Portland. Megan missed her family and the vibrant Portland food scene.

## Jeremy's Culinary Ascent

"My first job after culinary school was working as a dish washer. Those were the longest three months of my life," said Jeremy, whose family moved to the Portland area from Colorado when he was ten years old. Following high school, Jeremy attended Western Culinary School. Once Jeremy graduated from culinary school, he was ready to take on the world and become the head chef at a restaurant in Portland. No one ever accused Jeremy of lacking confidence. Getting hired to work as a dish washer was quite a shock. Humbled but not bowed, Jeremy began working his way up the Portland culinary ladder.

Of Megan, Jeremy said, "I never worked so well with anyone before [her]." Megan, in turn, said of Jeremy, "I love the way that [he] and I make food together." Within six months of beginning their relationship in 2007, Megan and Jeremy began talking about starting a culinary business together. They wanted to open a restaurant; however, they just did not have the financial resources for that. They eventually began talking about opening a food cart. Megan noted that "a food cart had the fewest barriers to entry."

## Christmas Meatballs!

When Megan was child, her Norwegian family would enjoy meatballs made from a family recipe at Christmas. The meatballs were topped with Gjetost ("yay-toast"). Gjetost is a decadent goat cheese sauce made from caramelized goat milk. The Gjetost that Megan enjoyed as a child, and that you can get today at Viking Soul Food, is Ekte Gjetost, or "true" Gjetost, and this means that the sauce is made *only* with goat milk and not cow's milk.

Years later, when Megan and Jeremy were invited to a Christmas party, Megan harkened back to those Christmas meatballs from her childhood. She made them and took them to the party. The meatballs covered in Gjetost were a huge hit. On the way home, Jeremy told Megan, "Let's sell those meatballs at a food cart!" Megan loved the idea and continued the concept, saying, "We can also have lefse and use them as a wrap for all kinds of things." With that, they had a cuisine. Now all they needed was a cart.

## The Fine Art of Making Lefse

Lesfe is a Norwegian flatbread that is made with potatoes that have been boiled and riced, butter, cream, salt and flour. This mixture is stirred, kneaded like bread dough, formed into patties and hand-rolled out to be very thin rounds about twelve inches or so in diameter. These rounds are then moved to a grill to be quickly cooked. After about thirty seconds, your lefse is ready to be flipped, and you need to use a lefse stick to effectively execute that delicate maneuver. Needless to say, lefse is very difficult to make. A fan named Susan Cersain

Gudrun, "She Who Knows the Secrets of Battle," at Viking Soul Food.

wrote on the VSF Facebook wall, "I grew up eating lefse every Christmas, but tonight I think I had the best lefse I've ever had."

Megan was four years old when she first got to make lefse with her grandma Clenora. It was Grandma Clenora who taught Megan to make lefse years ago, and Megan, in turn, was the one to teach Jeremy. I have had Jeremy's lefse, and while he may not be Norwegian, he sure can cook like one.

## Gudrun, "She Who Knows the Secrets of Battle"

In March 2010, Megan began looking on Craigslist for a food cart they could buy. Megan had started with Portland Craigslist, and she was just not finding what she wanted. Megan was on the hunt for a food cart that had character and charm. She expanded her search to include western Washington as well.

Finally, in Snoqualmie, Washington, she found a cart that she thought might work. On May 17, Norwegian Independence Day, Megan and Jeremy went to see it. Everything was perfect! The person selling the cart actually knew what lefse was, and she was delighted that her 1958 Streamline Duchess was going to be used for Norwegian cuisine.

When Megan and Jeremy went into their new cart for the first time, they found a picture of Julia Child on the wall. They took this to be a good sign. That picture is still up in the cart to this day. Megan and Jeremy brought their newly acquired food cart home to Portland and named it "Gudrun." They chose this name for two reasons. First, they loved what this Nordic name means ("she who knows the secrets of battle"). The second reason had to do with a successful Portland businesswoman who was friends with Megan's parents and who had inspired Megan as a teenager to believe that someday she could be a successful businesswoman herself.

Gudrun "Goody" Cable is the dynamic woman who is the founder and owner of the Rimsky-Korsakoffee House in Portland and the literary-themed Sylvia Beach Hotel in Newport, Oregon. Gudrun the Viking Soul Food Cart is named after her.

## While Having Martinis

Megan had been taking business classes at MercyCorps Northwest, and those classes drove home the point that their new business needed a name that was effective and memorable and reflected who they both were. In other words, the name they gave to their food cart business needed to fit with their brand story.

Megan was at her parents' having martinis when inspiration struck. She called Jeremy and excitedly told him, "I got it!" All she had to say were three words—"Viking Soul Food"—and Jeremy knew that their food cart business now had a name.

The first of those three words, "Viking," referred of course to Megan's Norwegian heritage, and the last two words, "Soul Food," were a tip of the hat to Jeremy's African American heritage. Megan and Jeremy felt that "soul food" not only referenced a type of cuisine that originated in African American culture but also evoked the idea that you could take the ingredients you had on hand and make food that was comforting and incredibly pleasing to the palate.

## They Just Walk Away

An interesting and sad phenomenon I have come across while talking with Portland food carts owners is something that Nimesh with Stumptown

Dumplings described this way: "People seem to want you to cook in your lane." Let me explain.

Timber Adamson is the founder of Timber's Doghouse PDX Food Cart. However, that is Timber's second food cart. She intentionally closed down her first food cart, which featured Korean food, because of the grief she received for being a white woman who was cooking authentic Korean food.

Justin and Nimesh sometimes get questions about their being Indian and having a food cart that sells Chinese dumplings. Jeremy has had similar experiences. More than once, Jeremy has seen an entire family—mom, dad, kids and even an aged grandma—come to the pod, walk right over to the prominent Viking Soul Food menu and began excitedly talking about the items on it.

In hushed, almost reverent voices, they say things like, "They *do* have lefse!…You can get lingonberries on your lefse—just like Grandma Jorun used to make…They have Gjetost!…Look—pickled herring!" People start naming off what they want to get, and someone starts keeping track of the dishes they are going to order. At that point, they look over to the cart window and see Jeremy's smiling face—his smiling *black* face. He has actually been asked, "Where is the viking?" Jeremy kindly answers, "She is not here right now, but I can help you." What they don't know is that Jeremy made that lefse and pickled that herring. In fact, his lefse is most likely way better than Grandma Jorun's ever was.

Once it sinks in that the only person in the cart is not Norwegian enough for them, they quietly confer with one another and then just walk away. My heart ached when Jeremy told me about these occurrences. It is incredibly painful to him when people who come to his food cart to enjoy his food end up walking away because of his skin color. Portland has the reputation as a liberal and progressive city. If Jeremy experiences that kind of racism here in my beloved city, I have to wonder what it is like in other parts of the country.

## Culinary Alchemists

One of the things I love the most about Viking Soul Food are the specials that Jeremy and Megan put on the menu. They are incredibly flavorful. Check out some of the lefse wraps they have served: the Winter Wrap, filled with roasted pears, Portland Creamery chèvre and sherry gastrique; the Ambrosia Wrap, with roasted peaches, Portland Creamery vanilla chèvre, walnuts and sherry syrup; the Polse, filled with chicken sausage, Jarlsberg cheese, mustard and lemon fennel slaw; and the Bird Brain, slow-cooked chicken, roasted mushrooms, asparagus, Jarlsberg cheese, walnuts and greens, all rolled into, you guessed it, a lefse. I could go on, but you get the picture.

The dish that convinced me that that these two chefs are culinary alchemists was when I had a simply delightful dish that included beets and vanilla. Who would ever think to combine beets and vanilla? As odd as it sounds, it was a really good dish. I am so glad that Grandma Clenora taught Megan to make lefse all these years ago.

*What's Next*: Megan and Jeremy would love to open up a brick-and-mortar Viking Soul Food restaurant some day. They would have an expanded menu, with plated entrées, and Megan has her heart set on having a fireplace with a large hearth. They also would like to have a small shop where people could buy lefse-making equipment and Scandinavian pastries and cookies that would be made right there in the kitchen.

*When You Go*: Come prepared to order a number of dishes. Of course, get an order of the pork and beef meatballs. They come with the Gjetost, that scrumptious sauce made from caramelized goat cheese. Get a sweet lefse with lingonberries and order a side of pickled herring. No really, order the pickled herring. Lastly, order whichever special most tickles your fancy.

*Recipes*: You can find three Viking Soul Food recipes (Lefse; Surkal, or sweet and sour cabbage; and Lemon Curd with Spiced Pecan Lefse) in *Trailer Food Diaries Cookbook*, Portland edition, vol. 1.

# A BAKER'S SENSE OF COOKING: PDX SIX SEVEN ONE

Ed Sablan opened the PDX Six Seven One Food Cart on May 25, 2010. Ed was born in Turkey and raised in Taguac, a community in the Guamanian village of Dededo, and now he is thriving in Portland. Here is his story.

Ed's parents are both Chamorro, and Ed's dad joined the U.S. Air Force. Ed was born in Turkey while his dad was stationed there. Chamorro is the name of the indigenous people of the Mariana Islands, which are located south of Japan and north of New Guinea, about 5,600 miles from Portland and 3,900 miles from Hawaii.

Ed graduated from Father Dueñas Memorial High School in 1993, and in August of that same year, he moved to Portland to pursue both an undergraduate degree and a very special woman named Marie. In 2000, Ed and Marie married.

## A Pizza Dough–Fueled Epiphany

Once Ed got to Portland, he proceeded to spend about seven years attending three different local colleges, each time taking classes related to art and/or music. Ed eventually found himself working at the McMenamins Kennedy School making pizza dough, and it was then that he remembered that he loved to bake. Ed had received his first baking cookbook in third grade, and he had done quite a bit of baking prior to high school.

The precision and science of baking deeply resonated with Ed, and he decided to attend culinary school. He graduated from Western Culinary Institute with a degree

Ed Sablan, owner of the PDX Six Seven One Food Cart.

149

in baking and patisserie. Even before he graduated, Ed was hired by St. Honoré Boulangerie, a prominent French bakery here in Portland.

Ed started at the bottom and worked his way up to production manager, and when St. Honoré Boulangerie opened its Lake Oswego location, it was Ed who oversaw the opening. At St. Honoré Boulangerie, Ed learned how to manage a culinary business.

## A Restaurant of His Own

Ed has wanted his own restaurant since he was a teenager living in Guam. Here in Portland, Ed would often find himself making the food he grew up enjoying in Guam for family and friends. He began to wonder, too, if maybe his dream to open his own restaurant could actually happen. In 2007, Ed decided that he would open a food cart featuring that cuisine, and he even bought the domain pdx671.com. PDX is the airport code for Portland, and 671 is the area code for Guam, though the business name uses "Six Seven One" officially.

## A Baker's Sense of Cooking

Really good bakers are meticulous, and they pay close attention to details, knowing that things like slight changes in humidity or room temperature can drastically effect what you are cooking. Ed began to apply that same approach to his dream to open PDX Six Seven One. In 2009, he quit his job and invested one year working full time on the business plan, menu and recipes for PDX Six Seven One.

## Chamorro Cuisine or Guamanian Cuisine?

The answer to this question is probably just "yes." On the PDX Six Seven One website, it mentions "Guamanian cuisine," and I have heard Ed talk about how the history of the Mariana Islands has shaped the cuisine the Chamorro people have grown up with. There are even differences between the cuisine of the Chamorro people from Guam and the cuisine of the Chamorro people from the northern Mariana Islands. Even though those two U.S. territories are only 128 miles apart, they each have had a very different history, and history affects flavor and food.

## Triple D

PDX Six Seven One has the honor of being the very first Portland food cart to ever be featured on Guy Fieri's Food Network show *Diners, Drive-Ins and Dives*. Ed is a very humble man, and he does not like to call attention to himself. Ed was both thrilled and a little uncomfortable to receive this honor.

## A Wonderful Ambassador

At the risk of embarrassing Ed, I have to say that he has done a stellar job of sharing the cuisine of his childhood with the world. Because Ed had the courage to pursue his dream, thousands of people now know about and enjoy items like Kelaguen Mannok, hineksa' agaga' and ensaladan kiukumba.

*What's Next*: Ed has a detailed plan to open up a **PDX Six Seven One** brick-and-mortar restaurant. Look for it sometime in 2015.

*When You Go*: Ed's most popular dish is the Kelaguen Mannok, a chopped, spicy grilled chicken that is served cold and features onions, grated coconut, chili peppers and lemon. My favorite dish at PDX Six Seven One is the Nengkanno' Gupot, or Fiesta Plate. This dish comes with a grilled chicken thigh that has been marinated overnight, red rice, shrimp fritters and Fina'dene', a Chamorro sauce that is made with soy sauce, lemon, chili peppers and onions. I also love the grilled chicken that comes with the Nengkanno' Gupot. It has a fantastic flavor that I have never had before, and it is some of the best barbecue chicken I have ever had. Whatever else you get at **PDX Six Seven One**, make sure that you get an order of Titiyas—hand-made, grilled, coconut milk flatbread. It is terrific and goes perfectly with every dish that Ed has on the menu.

*Recipes*: You can find two of PDX Six Seven One recipes (Kelaguen Mannok, chopped grilled chicken; and Boñelos Uhang, shrimp fritters) in *Trailer Food Diaries Cookbook*, Portland edition, vol. 2.

## PORTLAND'S ASIAN DUMPLING CHAMPS: STUMPTOWN DUMPLINGS

Justin Prasad and Nimseh Dayal launched the Stumptown Dumplings Food Cart on May 31, 2012. I was lucky enough to be at their grand opening that night, and I have been very impressed with the way they have grown their brand ever since.

They now have two food carts, one located at a food cart pod and a second mobile cart that is used for events and catering. They also have a service window location that is just down the wall from Voodoo Doughnuts and is open daily from 9:00 p.m. to 2:00 a.m., serving the late-night crowd. They will be opening a brick-and-mortar Stumptown Dumplings Restaurant in the first part of 2014. Not bad, not bad at all.

Nimesh Dayal and Justin Prasad, owners of the Stumptown Dumplings Food Cart.

## Fate Brought These Partners Together

Nimesh first came into Justin's life in 2000, when Nimesh began to date Jaishree, a friend of Justin's. When Jaishree became Nimesh's bride a year later, Justin was at that wedding. Within a few years, Justin and Nimesh drifted apart and lost touch.

Flash-forward to 2011. Justin is now the general manager of a restaurant, and he wants to open a food cart. He wants to have a business of his own to oversee and grow, and he is convinced that he can make a food cart business work. Later that same year, Justin is in the Pearl District at a bar for a birthday party. Lo and behold, Nimesh is there. He said to Justin, "We need to talk...I have been thinking about opening a food cart. Would you have any interest in partnering with me on a project like that?"

Justin remembered thinking, "Wow! What are the odds that I would run into Nimesh and that he would also want to open a food cart?" Justin had enough respect for Nimesh's business skill to seriously consider entering into a partnership with him. In Hindi, they call that "bhaagya." In English, we call that "fate" or "destiny." The funny thing is that in Gujarati, "bhaagya" means partnership.

Both Justin and Nimesh grew up here in the Portland area, and both are of Indian descent. Justin's family is from India via a two- to three-generational stopover in Fiji. Justin's second language is Fijian Hindi, which is similar to the traditional Hindi they speak in India. Nimesh's family is Gujarati, and his second language is Gujarati.

Bhaagya ("fate" in Hindi) brought them together into a bhaagya ("partnership" in Gujarati).

## The Last Hotel Had Been Sold

Nimesh had been working in his family's business. It is quite common for Gujarati to be involved in the hotel business. Some reports suggest that more than 40 percent of all motels in the United States are owned by Gujarati. The book *Life Behind the Lobby: Indian American Motel Owners and the American Dream* by Tufts University professor Pawan Dhingra chronicles this fascinating phenomenon.

Nimesh had overseen the business side of the hotels that his parents owned. They sold their last hotel and retired, and Nimseh needed to find something else to do. Succeeding as a food cart owner involves both culinary skills and business skills. Justin knew culinary, and Nimesh knew business. Sounds like bhaagya to me.

## *Making the Partnership Work*

Many partnerships don't end up working out. I have observed and been around Justin and Nimesh for more than a year and half now, and I have seen qualities that helped their partnership flourish. They have separate duties but the same goals. While their duties occasionally overlap, they tend to focus on their strengths. Nimesh is more of the business manager, and Justin is the head chef or chef de cuisine. This division of duties helps them avoid the problem that they playfully refer to as "too many chiefs and not enough Indians."

## *Liquid Gold*

I would be remiss if I did not mention the fantastic Liquid Gold Thai Iced Tea they have at Stumptown Dumplings. I love it, and my two younger sons, Zac and Zayne, consider it their hands-down favorite beverage of all time. I am very lucky that you can't yet get take-home growlers of that Thai iced tea. If they could, Zac and Zayne would drink it by the gallon.

The Stumptown Dumplings Food Cart.

Justin spent quite a bit of time perfecting his Thai iced tea recipe. He said that he can't stand it when you order a Thai iced tea, and you taste the milk and the sugar rather than the tea itself. The Thai iced tea at Stumptown has that distinctive tea flavor that comes through very nicely.

## Chinese Dumplings and Boa

Thai iced tea aside, the dumplings and boa really are the stars of show at Stumptown Dumplings. Every once in a while, Justin and Nimesh get asked, "What are you guys doing cooking Chinese dumplings?" Once someone tastes one of their dumplings, that question is completely answered.

Regularly, Justin and Nimesh are told things like, "I used to live in Hong Kong, and these are the best dumplings I've had since living there!" As one fan wrote on the Stumptown Dumplings Facebook wall, "Best I've had outside of Beijing. Just phenomenally great." I encourage you to go check out Stumptown Dumplings and see for yourself why it is Portland's Asian Dumpling champ.

*What's Next*: Justin and Nimesh are going to open the Stumptown Dumplings brick-and-mortar restaurant in the first half of 2014. I am hoping that their new restaurant will have a bar so that I can enjoy some Thai iced tea cocktails. I can think of a number of ways to make a great cocktail using Stumptown Dumplings Thai iced tea. One of my ideas is to add coconut rum to the tea. Once the restaurant is open, Justin and Nimesh hope to bottle three of their sauces for retail sale—the Asian chipotle, the Thai mustard and the chili hoisin.

*When You Go*: I love the chicken dumplings with the creamy peanut sauce. Get a coconut custard bao for dessert. Lastly, make sure that you get some of that Thai iced tea.

*Recipes*: You can find a recipe for Stumptown Dumplings' Thai iced tea and Asian Chipotle Sauce in *Trailer Food Diaries Cookbook*, Portland edition, vol. 2.

# OUT OF EGYPT: RAMY'S LAMB SHACK

*Far, We've been traveling far. Without a home, but not without a star. Free. Only want to be free. We huddle close. Hang on to a dream. On the boats and on the planes, they're coming to America. Never looking back again, They're coming to America. Home...To a new and a shiny place. Make our bed and we'll say our grace. Freedom's light burning warm, Freedom's light burning warm.*

*—Neil Diamond, 1981*

Ramy Armans opened the Ramy's Lamb Shack Food Cart in March 2012. With this step, he fulfilled his childhood dream of being self-employed. I am inspired by the fact that eleven years earlier, Ramy arrived in the United States as a seventeen-year-old kid with no assets to his name other than an unwavering belief in the American dream.

Ramy Armans, owner of the Ramy's Lamb Shack Food Cart.

156

Ramy was born and grew up in Cairo, Egypt. He was born into a Christian family, and as early as he can remember, the members of his family were persecuted for following the "wrong" religion. Ramy remembered being a small child and watching while an adult family member was kidnapped off the street in front of him, shoved into a minivan and taken away. It was weeks before that family member was returned home, having been severely beaten and abused—all because the family were not Muslim and worshiped Jesus rather than Allah. Some people in America read about religious persecution and feel for those in such situations, while others aren't sure if it's really that bad "over there." But it is that bad. Just ask Ramy what it was like to grow up Christian in a Muslim country.

In America, the Constitution provides for religious freedom. If you were born a Minnesota Lutheran, you can move to San Francisco and become a Buddhist. Not only can you do that, it is perfectly legal to do so. In many Muslim countries, the law of the land declares it a crime punishable by death to convert from Muslim to Christianity.

The stanza from Emma Lazarus's poem adorning the bronze plaque on the Statue of Liberty is a fitting reminder of those who leave one home to find another:

> *Give me your tired, your poor,*
> *Your huddled masses yearning to breathe free,*
> *The wretched refuse of your teeming shore.*
> *Send these, the homeless, tempest-tost to me,*
> *I lift my lamp beside the golden door!*

There were two bright spots in Ramy's childhood. The first was cooking with his mom. He began cooking at an early age and loved working with spices and trying new combinations. The second was the hope that someday his family could move to the land of the free and the home of the brave.

Ramy yearned to move to America, a place where he could have the freedom to publicly practice his faith and be able to start his own business. Ramy knew that in Egypt, it would very difficult, if not impossible, for him to be a native-born Egyptian man *and* a Christian, as well as have the self-employment success that he dreamed about.

It was a plane that brought Ramy to America, and after a brief layover at Dulles International Airport, he landed at PDX to begin a new life. His first job was at a gas station at 181st and Burnside. Eventually, Ramy went to work as a meat cutter at the Winco grocery chain, where he learned skills that would later serve him well in his food cart. From there, Ramy went into retail management, working at both Best Buy and OfficeMax.

In 2007, Ramy began going to the SW 9th and Alder food cart pod. There he began to think that maybe a food cart would be the way he could start his own business. Ramy even began running spreadsheets in 2007 to try to figure out what it would take to succeed as a food cart owner.

## What Do You Want to Do?

In 2009, Ramy met Leila Ramezani, a beautiful woman who grew up in Tehran, Iran. Leila had her own story of her journey to the United States, immigrating here with her family in 2001. Leila quickly became his girlfriend, and in 2010, she asked Ramy, "What do you want to do?" Ramy had a good corporate job, but his desire to have his own business left him feeling restless. Ramy told Leila that he had wanted to be self-employed since he was child, as well as that he thought that he could do it by opening a food cart.

Leila said, "Well, you should do it. I believe in you." From that moment on, Ramy began making plans to open his food cart. The first cart that Ramy bought was not especially attractive, to put it mildly. He paid $3,500 for it and spent months renovating it. It was ugly, but it was his. As Ramy says, "The American dream is real. You have to bust your ass, believe in yourself and work for it. Do those things and you can make it!"

Ramy eventually replaced his first food cart with a newer, much better-looking one, and within less than a year, he had opened his second food cart. In December 2012, when he was tearing down that first cart, Ramy became so overcome with emotion that he sat down and cried. He realized that he had come a long way from the dusty streets of Cairo, where he wished that he could be free and have his own business. That first cart, ugly as it was, had helped his dream come true.

It drives Ramy crazy to hear people born in America complain about the lack of opportunity. He does not understand people who were lucky enough to be born here and yet complain about their life instead of working to improve it. If you ask Ramy about this, he will passionately tell you that in America, if you want to better yourself, you can, but only with hard work and determination.

By the way, Ramy and Leila were married on October 14, 2013, on the beach in Maui, Hawaii.

*What's Next*: Ramy plans to continue to build his brand, and he has a number of plans for how to expand it, including opening up a brick-and-mortar restaurant someday.

*When You Go*: Get a lamb kabob and a chicken gyro—both are wonderful. For dessert, get some of Ramy's signature baklava. My grandmother first introduced me to baklava when I was small child, and I have loved it ever since. I have enjoyed it all over the world, including places like Thessaloniki, Greece, and Los Angeles, California, and Ramy's baklava is the best I have ever had.

*Recipes*: You can find the Ramy's Lamb Shack recipe for Beef and Lamb Kofta in *Trailer Food Diaries Cookbook*, Portland edition, vol. 1.

# MORE FULFILLED THAN I HAVE EVER BEEN: BENTO BOX

Jeff and Madeline Mendon opened the Bento Box Food Cart in the dead of winter in January 2013. In the course of one short year, Bento Box has developed numerous fans and attracted a plethora of people who consider themselves part of the Bento Box community. In other words, they have succeeded as a startup, they have established a great brand and they are the proud owners of a successful, thriving food cart in downtown Portland. How have they succeeded where so many others have failed?

One of the most interesting aspects of their food cart success story is that unlike many food cart owners, they had *no* previous professional culinary experience. Jeff worked in the medical device field, and Madeline is an elementary school teacher.

## *Choosing Portland*

Jeff and Madeline both grew up in California. They met each other at Chico State University, which is located ninety miles north of Sacramento. They finished college, married and moved to Redwood City, California. Right out of college, Jeff talked about opening a restaurant. He really wanted to do this. And then, as he put it, "life happened," and that dream got put on the shelf.

Jeff and Madeline Mendon, owners of the Bento Box Food Cart.

They lived in Redwood City for four years, and it never felt like home. They did lots of research on where they might want to live and raise their family. They picked the Pacific Northwest, and it came down to Seattle and Portland. They visited Seattle and really liked it. Then they visited Portland and liked this city even more. In 1990, they both quit their jobs and moved to Portland. They had come "home."

## The Portland Food Scene

Both Madeline and Jeff are foodies. They watched the Portland food scene develop and eventually flourish over the next twenty years. They ate at and loved most of the restaurants that people around the country read about. They were true fans of the local scene.

Along the way, as each of those twenty years rolled by, Jeff would wistfully remember his long-ago dream to open a restaurant of his own. Jeff and Madeline would sit in those amazing Portland restaurants and talk with each other and dream about how much fun it would be to not just be fans of the Portland food scene but to actually be a part of it.

In 2003, Jeff began to think about opening a food cart of his own. He did not have the financial resources necessary to open a restaurant. Maybe, just maybe, a food cart was a viable way to finally stretch his culinary wings. Things started to come together for Jeff and Madeline's culinary dreams in 2010. By then, Jeff had decided on the name, concept and menu for his food cart.

## Bento

*Bento* is the Japanese name for a takeout or home-packed meal for one. A traditional bento has rice, meat (or fish) and vegetables. Jeff became convinced that a food cart that served simple, healthy food with a limited menu would work here in Portland. Jeff loved bento, and he loved grilled chicken, so he decided that his food cart would serve what he loved.

Keeping with the "simple" theme, Jeff and Madeline decided to call their food cart Bento Box. Their cart now had a name, a concept and a menu. Just a few more pieces of the puzzle were needed.

## More than Six Years in the Making

The cart-made teriyaki sauce served at Bento Box is not a glaze; it is a light sauce that Jeff invested many years perfecting. This teriyaki sauce was a hit right from the get-go. As soon as Bento Box opened, Madeline encouraged Jeff to hand out samples of his teriyaki sauce. Jeff revels in the weekly expletives he receives. Someone will sample his teriyaki sauce for the first time and exclaim, "F@#%!...I need to get me some of that."

With the teriyaki sauce recipe finalized, all they needed was a cart and a location for that cart.

## *Finding a Food Cart*

In December 2012, Jeff saw a food cart for lease on Craigslist on Alder, just past 10th. They had been looking for a food cart near 10th and Alder. Jeff spent a few hours considering this location before he picked up the phone to try to lease this cart. By the time Jeff called, the cart had already been taken.

The very next week, Jeff saw another ad on Craigslist for a food cart for lease. This time, the cart was right on 10th between Alder and Washington. Jeff immediately picked up the phone. He was not going to let this cart slip through his fingers.

Fricken Good Chicken at the Bento Box Food Cart.

Madeline remembered driving with Jeff to their prospective cart to meet the person they would be leasing from. Would this be it? After ten years of planning, would they finally have a food cart business to call their own? After more than twenty years of dreaming, would they actually become part of the Portland food scene?

Yes, yes and yes. They signed a lease for that food cart, and they were ready to open their window and offer their version of bento to the world.

## *Paying the Price*

In the process of getting Bento Box up and running, Jeff had to quit his corporate job. Coworkers told him that he was "completely out of his mind." In his first summer, Jeff worked sixteen to eighteen hours per day, and he was open seven days a week. In its first spring and fall, Bento Box was open six days a week, and Jeff put in twelve-hour days.

I asked Jeff what it feels like to work that hard. He said, "At the end of the day, my whole body hurts, especially my wrists, my knees and my back. I come home bone tired. And…I wake up excited to get out of bed and do it again. I am more fulfilled than I have ever been."

*What's Next*: Jeff and Madeline would love to see their food cart brand grow to the place where a brick-and-mortar Bento Box is feasible. I have strongly encouraged them to look into bottling Jeff's teriyaki sauce. I know that I would regularly buy it if I could.

*When You Go*: Get a Chicken Bento Box. They really do have "Fricken Good Chicken." The grilled chicken is incredible. Make sure that you get yours with extra teriyaki sauce. Trust me on this this: Jeff's teriyaki sauce will be some of the best teriyaki sauce you have ever tasted.

# Food Writer's Perspective:
## AARON WAKAMATSU

Aloha! I'm Aaron Wakamatsu, the man behind Aaron's Food Adventures, a blog that I started back in May 2011. Originally, I intended my food blog to be a simple private journal to document the places I went to for food. Over time, my blog gained a following that includes many Portland food cart owners.

I launched a YouTube channel in August 2012 to expand the scope of my audience. Today, I have followers worldwide. I usually do two to three blog posts and two to three videos per week. I am very active on social media, so be sure to follow my adventures. I just might show up in your town!

I grew up in Hawaii on the island of Oahu. Not many people might know that Hawaii also has a long history in the food cart scene. Many of us growing up on the islands have known them as "lunch wagons," as these owners usually served the general public during lunch hour.

Although I have lived in the Pacific Northwest since 2007, I did not realize that Portland had a bustling food cart scene until 2010. I was going to school in Salem, Oregon, at the time, and one of my classmates said that I had to check out the Portland food carts one day.

People have told me that it is their dream to go to Hawaii for the food and the culture. Interestingly, those are the reasons I love staying in and around Portland. Like Hawaii, Portland has become a melting pot of delicious dishes from around the world. Where else in the United States can you find food carts offering dishes from Guam, Poland, Ethiopia, Mauritius, Russia and the country of Georgia within the city limits?

With more than five hundred food carts open for business in Portland at any one time, I've been asked what sets one food cart apart from the others. First, I look at the personality of the food cart owner or the employee running the cart. A simple "Hi," "Thank you" or a smile goes a long way. I believe that the person should be full of energy and doing anything possible to make the customer feel welcome. To me, Todd Edwards at Olé Latte Coffee is a prime example of a charismatic individual. I have visited his cart multiple times just to get a coffee and chat with the man for a few minutes. Frankly, we need more food cart owners like him.

Second, a great Portland cart has delicious, addicting food. Just about everyone I know has a favorite dish or finds something on the menu that sounds incredible. Think of something you ate one day that you still dream about many months or years later.

Finally, I believe that a great food cart has that "it factor" or some other intangible that innately makes you keep coming back. It is a purely subjective criterion unique to each individual.

Here are some of my top Portland food cart dishes, those menu items that have stood out and left an indelible mark on my palate:

Original Breakfast Tacos from the Pepper Box: Jim Wilson brought the flavors of New Mexico to Portland, including adding New Mexico green chile and red chile to various menu items. Breakfast lovers will enjoy the abundance of cage-free eggs, potatoes and cheddar cheese. The best part: Jim makes his own flour tortillas from scratch.

The Dirty Mo's Super Q Pulled Pork Sandwich from J-Mo's Sandwich Shack: While "J-Mo" and others flock first to the "Dirty Mo" sandwich (think spaghetti and meatballs inside garlic cheese bread), I got hooked on J-Mo's massive pulled pork sandwich that should satisfy the hungriest of appetites. Heaps of tender, juicy, slow-roasted pulled pork inside a roll, topped with sweet-tangy barbecue sauce. I highly recommend adding the homemade coleslaw for added crunch.

Chicharron Sandwich from La Sangucheria: Maribel, owner of this Peruvian food cart, recently won the Judges' Choice Award at Eat Mobile 2013. The honor is even more significant when competing against at least fifty other carts for the coveted crown. Here, "chicharron" is not simply fried pork skin but rather skin-on slices of seasoned pork loin hitting the deep fryer. The exterior crisps up slightly to leave me wanting more. The refreshing sarza criolla, a South American salsa featuring sliced red onions, cilantro and habaneros, tickled my taste buds and blew my mind.

Kelaguen Mannok from PDX Six Seven One: Ed and Marie Sablan provided my first introduction to Guamanian food. Their version of Kelaguen Mannok is more than a cold chicken salad; it simply makes me feel like I'm enjoying a fabulous meal in Guam. While the minced bird's eye chili tickles my taste buds, the refreshing lemon in the dish provides the extra bite and makes this dish pop. Enjoy Kelaguen Mannok with their signature hineksa' agaga' (red rice) or titiyas (flatbread), plus some finadene' (a Chamorro sauce) on the side. Not surprisingly, this food cart was featured on Guy Fieri's *Diners, Drive-Ins and Dives* in September 2013. I couldn't be happier for Ed and Marie. *Si yu'os ma'ase* (thank you) for bringing Guamanian cuisine to Portland!

People should experience the world of Portland food carts at least once in their lifetimes. Even after three years, my food adventures are still just beginning. Perhaps I will see you at a Portland food cart in the near future.

# PART VII

# COMFORT FOOD

## CHEESE MAKES ME HAPPY:
## HERB'S MAC & CHEESE

Herb Acken opened Herb's Mac and Cheese Food Cart in January 2011 after having moved from Florida to Portland in the fall of 2010. Herb had originally intended to sell his mac and cheese at the Portland Saturday Market the first part of the 2011 and then open his food cart in the spring.

When Herb got to Portland, he discovered that the Portland Saturday Market was closed the first two months of the year for its winter break, and he realized that he couldn't go two months without income, so he decided to get his cart open right away.

Herb was able to get his cart configured for making his intended menu, and he found an open spot at the now defunct D-Street Noshery Food Cart Pod at 32$^{nd}$ and Division, and he was off and running.

Herb noted, "I like the rain. I was a lifeguard on the beach for fifteen years. I am good with less UV." Prior to his big move, Herb had lived in Fort Myers, Florida. While there, he owned a few businesses, including the EB Café, an outside-seating-only restaurant called Burrito a Go Go and a shaved ice cart. He spent his last two years in Florida selling shaved ice right on the beach.

Herb's Mac & Cheese Food Cart. *Photo by Molly Woodstock.*

When Herb left Florida, he brought his shaved ice cart with him. He changed the graphics and the equipment and added some diner blocks across the top. What was once a cart on a beach was now a Portland food cart.

For Herb, it was time for a change, and Portland had everything that he wanted, including "rainy weather and beautiful scenery." For Herb, Portland was a place that "encourages those with an entrepreneurial spirit."

## Why Such a Creative Name?

Herb chose to call his food cart Herb's Mac & Cheese. He had learned the hard way that the name of your business should clearly communicate to people what it is, as well as what you sell. Back in Florida, he had many people think that Burrito a Go Go only sold burritos to go. He also got very tired of people jokingly asking, "Do your burritos make you go?"

## The First Year

I asked Herb how many hours per week he worked his first year. He answered, "All of them." That first year, Herb worked mostly seven days a week and put in seventy to eighty hours per week—some weeks even more than that.

## Vegan Mac and Cheese with Bacon

Herb sells a tofu-based vegan "cheese" sauce, and he sells quite a bit of it. He still remembers the first time someone ordered bacon with the vegan mac and cheese. Herb was very confused and could not help but give his customer a double take. She told him, "I am not a vegan. I am lactose-intolerant." It is common for people to order his vegan mac and cheese with one of the meat toppings that Herb offers.

## Build Your Own!

At Herb's Mac & Cheese, you can add a number of awesome toppings to your dish: baked breadcrumbs, chicken, hot dogs, garlic, broccoli, sun-dried tomatoes, feta crumbles and blue cheese crumbles. I have two favorite combinations. The first is chicken, Frank's Red Hot Cayenne Pepper Sauce and blue cheese crumbles. The second is mushroom, feta cheese and bacon. The beauty of Herb's menu is that you can build whatever you want.

## Why Mac and Cheese?

Herb had made his signature mac and cheese for family for years, and it was always greeted with rave reviews. When it came time to choose a cuisine for his food cart, mac and cheese won for a number of reasons. He believed that mac and cheese fit Portland and was convinced that Portland would support such a food cart. To Herb, mac and cheese is quintessential comfort food, and he loved the idea of selling comfort food. Most importantly, Herb said, "Cheese just makes me happy." The idea of having a business where he could pass on that happiness sounded perfect to him.

Herb Acken, owner of Herb's Mac & Cheese Food Cart. *Photo by Molly Woodstock.*

*What's Next*: Herb gets many requests to package and sell his vegan cheese sauce, and he is looking into doing that. He would also love to someday open up a brick-and-mortar Herb's Mac & Cheese. He would serve his mac and cheese in small cast-iron skillets and add breadsticks, cheesy breadsticks, beer and wine to his list of offerings.

*When You Go*: Pick the toppings that resonate with you and enjoy some of the best mac and cheese you will ever have.

# MORE THAN JUST A BAKER: THE SUGAR SHOP

Autumn Burns and Shannon Scully opened the Sugar Shop Food Cart in August 2012, and with this step, they were finally professional bakers. They were finally "making cookies for a living." So many people want to do something different with their life and don't because of fear, doubt or peer pressure/family pressure to take the "traditional" route. I am very fond of these two courageous women, and I am honored to share their story.

## *What Does Your Heart Say*

Autumn attended Louisiana State University and graduated with a degree in kinesiology. The goal was medical school. Autumn took some time off from that path once graduation was over. One thing led to another, and she ended up back in her home state of New Mexico dating a chef who had been to culinary school.

Autumn came to realize that if she could, she would become a baker. The question was not whether she could become a baker. The question was whether she would allow herself to. Up to this point, she had been pursuing one of those careers that parents brag about—doctor, lawyer and so on.

Who wants to say, "I was going to be doctor, but now I roll dough out for a living?" I will tell you who—people who love to roll dough. Sometimes, when faced with this tough kind of crossroad, people say no to the dream that smolders in their heart and pursue the career that they think they should.

The sad news is that you can't extinguish those kinds of dreams. They just keep burning and are always there. Unpursued dreams keep burning in your heart, and eventually they become a dull, ongoing ache.

## Not Doctor or a Lawyer—Just a Baker

Autumn wrestled with the fear of being "just a baker"—baker is not one of those cool careers. Thankfully, when she talked to her mom, her mom got it and affirmed the idea that Autumn should pursue her dream, even if it wasn't as cool as being a doctor. Autumn and that chef she was in love with headed off to Portland so Autumn could attend the Oregon Culinary Institute and become a baker. This chef who believed in Autumn's dream is named Jason. He's a great chef and an even better guy. I hope that my daughters end up with someone as awesome as he is.

"I have wanted to be a baker as long as I can remember," said Shannon Scully. Before moving to Portland in 2011, Shannon had a tough journey. One constant was her love of baking. In her late teens, Shannon got a job at a bakery working in the front as a barista. She was finally able to convince the owner to let her go to the back to bake. Shannon loved it, even though the person who was the head baker spoke no English—Shannon's first lessons in professional baking came via hand signals.

Later, Shannon entered culinary school in San Francisco and made it three-fourths of the way through. Things did not work out, and one day Shannon left and never went back. At this point, most people would have given up on their dreams. Shannon kept battling for her dream, and a few years later, she moved to Portland to attend her second culinary school: the Oregon Culinary Institute.

## The Very First Week

Autumn and Shannon met at OCI their first week. Both of them had been in Oregon less than a week, and they both were there to become bakers. They became fast friends and discovered that they had much in common. They both love the rain. They both love Portland "for the food, the vegetables, the neighborhoods and the wine." Both of them remembered baking for the first time as a small child, making chocolate chip cookies with mom. They both have very quirky senses of humor. Most importantly, both of them love to bake. As Autumn said, "You know that you are a baker if, when you are really stressed out, you bake." Shannon added, "There is something very therapeutic about rolling dough."

## *Cinco de Mayo 2012*

Jason was working, and Autumn and Shannon found themselves together on Thursday night, May 5, 2012, drinking margaritas. It was during that evening that they decided to open a food cart together. They knew that they could work together because they "are both really not nice people."

Actually, they *are* both very nice people. They just prefer to be blunt and direct. To me, that is part of their charm. I also like it that when I am around them, I can be more open and not filter myself so much. They both revel in the fact that they have a business partner with whom they can have the freedom to be very honest. They have a great working relationship.

The Sugar B's: Autumn Burns and Shannon Scully, owners of the Sugar Shop Food Cart.

## The Boozy Bakers

Both Shannon and Autumn love to bake with booze. They love the challenge, the creativity and the science. While all of their desserts are truly amazing, the ones made with booze are on a whole other level. To get an idea of what these incredible bakers can do, here are some the desserts that I have enjoyed from their food cart: chocolate chip bacon cookies, cheddar biscuits filled with cart-made bacon jam, strawberry cake topped with basil buttercream and balsamic drizzle, pumpkin bourbon mousse on a nutmeg shortbread, lemon cake with cranberry Riesling compote and chocolate cake with a goat cheese frosting and port drizzle.

## The Sugar B's Can Flat-Out Bake

Early on in their food cart journey, Autumn and Shannon were given the nickname "the Sugar B's." You will have to ask them about this nickname. While you are at it, ask them about the eye patch of shame, fruit box shoes, yogurt yeti and dormant mayonnaise. Remember, they spend many hours a day in a little metal box baking. Sometimes I think that they go a little mad. But who wants a completely sane baker anyway?

I am so glad that each of them had the guts to battle for her dream to become a baker. To me, Autumn and Shannon are not "just bakers." They are the kind of inspiration that the world needs to know about.

*What's Next*: Autumn and Shannon are working on a cookbook, and someday they would like to have a brick-and-mortar business that has the Sugar Shop bakery on one side and the Sugar B's Bar on the other. The bakery would be open during the day and have cakes, pies, scones, cookies and so on. The Sugar B's Bar would be open nights and have cocktails and the boozy bakers' signature desserts for grown-ups.

*When You Go*: The menu is seasonal. Everything is mind-blowingly good. Just order four or five items and worry about your diet tomorrow.

*Recipes*: You can find three of the Sugar Shop recipes (Ginger Carrot Cake with Orange Cream Cheese Frosting; Lemon Cake; and Molasses Spice Cookies) in *Trailer Food Diaries Cookbook*, Portland edition, vol. 2.

# TENACITY AND ARTISTRY: GAUFRE GOURMET

Charlene and Michael opened the Gaufre Gourmet Food Cart on November 22, 2010, a day they consider to be the worst possible day to open your food cart. In 2010, November 22 was the Monday before Thanksgiving. Their opening-day sales totaled three dollars, but they have come a long way since then.

## *While Watching the Travel Channel*

Michael and Charlene met in 2008. They were both working for a catering company. They became a couple shortly after that first meeting. By 2009, the catering company they worked for had become severely affected by the economic crash that affected so many of us. They knew that eventually both of them would be laid off.

Michael and Charlene decided that maybe opening a food cart together would be a viable economic path for them to take. The next decision they

needed to make was deciding what cuisine they would sell at this food cart.

Michael Susak and Charlene Wesler, owners of the Gaufre Gourmet Food Cart.

174

On Wednesday, May 13, 2009, Charlene and Michael were watching the Travel Channel, and they learned about Liège-style waffles. Nothing was ever the same after that, but more on Liège-style waffles in a bit. A few days later, they decided that they were going to open a food cart selling these specialty waffles. Michael and Charlene began researching how to make Liège waffles. They got a waffle iron and spent the next year perfecting their recipe. In May 2010, they purchased and began to renovate their food cart.

## That Tree Is a Deal-Breaker

Michael and Charlene began looking for a place to put their food cart. They really wanted to be downtown at the 9th and Alder food cart pod. A spot there opened, and they went to look at it. Unfortunately, there was a tree that would be right in front of their cart, and Charlene vetoed this otherwise perfect spot.

## The Tenacity to Press On

They ended up at 4th and Burnside. That pod got closed down in June 2011, and they had to move, this time to the Green Castle Food Cart Pod just off 19th and Burnside. That pod was not a good match for their cuisine. Sales were awful, and they almost went out of business. Then that pod closed down, and they had to move again. "There were so many times that first year that we could have quit and many more times that we wondered if maybe we should," said Charlene.

They were now a year into their food cart business. They hadn't really made any money, and they needed to move their cart for the third time. I asked Michael why they did not simply throw in the towel and find something else to do. Michael said that they believed in their product and knew that if they persisted, they would reach a tipping point where they had enough fans to sustain their business.

## The Tree Is Back

They heard that a spot for a food cart had opened up on 9th and Alder—the pod they had originally wanted to be at. They were very hopeful as they quickly hurried to see if they could secure it. As they approached the open spot, Charlene realized that this was the exact same spot she had vetoed more than a year ago. The tree was still there. You can see that tree when you visit Gaufre Gourmet because it is right in front of their cart. Charlene was not going to let a tree stand in the way of their dream.

## Culinary Artistry

Michael loved the idea of serving Liège-style waffles because it takes real culinary skill to pull them off. The artistry required appealed to him. Liège waffles are not made from batter. They are made from a yeasted dough that you have to first let rise for two hours or so. Next, you punch the dough down and let it rise for a second time. Finally, you have to portion it off, and then you are ready for the waffle iron—assuming, of course, that you have the right one.

To make authentic Liège-style waffles, you need a special cast-iron waffle iron that weighs one hundred pounds and takes from thirty to forty-five minutes to heat up. Lastly, you need to use a decadent substance known as Pearl Sugar. Pearl Sugar is a coarse, hard sugar that caramelizes when it encounters the heat of the waffle iron. Unless your grandma is Belgian, these waffles are not your grandma's waffles. These are way better.

## The Smell Will Lure You In

There is nothing quite like the smell of these waffles as they are being cooked. The appealing aroma will grab ahold of you and not let go! Don't resist. Just follow your nose and be prepared to become enraptured in culinary ecstasy. These waffles are chewy and tender at the same time. And they are finished with a sprinkling of vanilla powered sugar.

## Gow-Free?

*Gaufre* is a French word that means "waffles." I have heard many Portlanders pronounce this word "gow-free." I have watched a director with the Food Network who had a French background painfully cringe when he heard this pronunciation. I have been told that you can pronounce this word with a few acceptable variations: "go-ff," "go-f-fray" or "go-f-fra." The nice thing is that Charlene and Mike don't care how you pronounce it. They just want you to enjoy their amazing waffles!

## No One Will Want Goat Cheese on a Waffle

Gaufre Gourmet has a very innovative menu. You can get a classic waffle (my favorite), and you can get a waffle drizzled with Belgian chocolate sauce and topped with whipped cream. You can also get the Milk and Honey Waffle—topped with goat cheese mousse, honey-roasted pistachios and balsamic caramel sauce.

When Carlene first suggested adding this waffle to the menu, Michael was sure that it was a bad idea. He was convinced that no one would want goat cheese on a waffle. He also opposed the Monte Cristo and the Spicy Goat. All three are top sellers, and Charlene came up with all three of those winners.

The Monte Cristo has turkey, ham, Swiss cheese and strawberry preserves, all on a waffle. I knew that I would love the Monte Cristo even before I tasted it. Disneyland was one of the few bright spots in my childhood, and I loved getting to have lunch at the Blue Bayou Restaurant that is inside the Pirates of the Caribbean attraction. I had a Monte Cristo sandwich for lunch at the Blue Bayou many times. I was delighted to discover that Charlene had been inspired by her own visits to the Blue Bayou! Her version does not disappoint.

The Spicy Goat is a waffle topped with arugula, chèvre cheese, pistachios, salami and Kelly's habanero jelly. This waffle is spicy and sweet and perfect. It is so good that it helped Gaufre Gourmet beat out more than fifteen other food carts for the grand prize at the 2013 Summer Portland Food Cart Festival. When you visit Gaufre Gourmet, make sure to ask to see the trophy.

## Courage and Creativity

Michael and Charlene had the courage to keep pursuing their food cart dream even when the outlook sometimes looked very bleak that first year. They also had the creativity to combine things like goat cheese and balsamic caramel sauce and put them on a waffle. I applaud their tenacity and artistry.

*What's Next*: Michael and Charlene have a number of big dreams, including a second food cart for events and catering, opening a brick-and-mortar location and packaging some of their items.

*When You Go*: No matter what else you get from Gaufre Gourmet, buy yourself the Original. It is simple elegance. The Original is one of my all-time favorite dishes. I also love the Milk and Honey Waffle, the Monte Cristo and the Maple Bacon Waffle.

*Recipes*: You can find the Gaufre Gourmet recipe for ABC Waffle—Arugula, Bacon and Camembert with Fig Sauce—in *Trailer Food Diaries Cookbook*, Portland edition, vol. 1. Three more of Gaufre Gourmet's recipes (Chèvre Mousse; Balsamic Caramel Sauce; and Buttermilk Biscuit Waffle Dough) can be found in *Trailer Food Diaries Cookbook*, Portland edition, vol. 2.

# RUGBY, NOT SOCCER: TIMBER'S DOGHOUSE PDX

Timber Adamson has been a food cart owner since April 1, 2010. She opened Timber's Doghouse PDX in its current configuration on April 1, 2012. Her journey has taken her from Springdale, Arkansas, to Portland, Oregon, with important stops in Fayetteville, Chicago and Korea. Each of those stops along the way has led her to where she is now.

Timber graduated from Western Culinary School here in Portland in 2006. She went to culinary school so she could become self-employed and work in molecular gastronomy. In case you were wondering, her food cart does not sell hot dogs. The Doghouse PDX (aka Timber's Doghouse PDX) sells some of the best hamburgers you will ever have. Trust me, it all makes sense.

## *Ice Does Cut: Becoming Timber*

Timber grew up in Springdale, Arkansas, and while growing up, she enjoyed a life-changing hamburger, but more on that important hamburger in a minute. Timber had a different first name until college. In college, she played rugby for the University of Arkansas. In that sport, when you make your first try (a score), you are expected to "Zulu"—to strip down naked and run around the field. When Timber scored her first try, she was too shy to strip down right on the pitch (field) in front of the fans and the other team.

Timber's team told her that she could Zulu at a later date. The date was picked, and the time was set for the middle of the night. As fate would have it, there was an ice storm preceding the selected date, and the pitch was a sheet of ice. Timber dutifully stripped down to just her cleats and proceeded to run across the pitch—she immediately fell and slid across the ice. Timber shivered a little when she told me this story, and she ended it by saying, "Ice does cut." I left that comment alone.

At the very next practice, while doing a common rugby drill, Timber tripped herself up and fell down once again. At the end of practice, her whole team lined up and called out to her, and all of them proceeded to fall over, each one yelling, "Timberrr!" From that day on, Ms. Adamson had a brand-new first name.

To this day, Timber loves rugby, and she played here in Portland in 2007 and 2008, on an Oregon Sports Union (ORSU) rugby team.

## *The Rain, the Produce and Safety*

Timber eventually left Arkansas for Portland to attend culinary school. When she was considering culinary school, she had three options: Scottsdale, Arizona; Atlanta, Georgia; and Portland. Portland won for two reasons: Timber was done with being in the hot sun, and Portland had the best produce. When she got here, she discovered a wonderful third benefit to Portland. Here in Portland, Timber felt safe for the first time in her adult life.

Timber found that Portland was a place where people accepted you for who you were and where her sexual orientation was not an issue. In Arkansas, Timber had not ever felt safe. As we sat at a picnic table next

Timber Adamson, owner of the Timber's Dog House PDX Food Cart.

to her food cart, Timber told me some of the experiences she had had in Arkansas, and I cried. No one should have to go through the things that she did.

## Chicago and Korea

Following culinary school, Timber had an externship at Alinea, a Chicago restaurant started by Grant Achatz, the leading American chef in molecular gastronomy. Upon returning to Portland, she followed a girlfriend to Korea, where she spent almost two years. In Korea, Timber fell in love with Korean food, and she spent day and night applying both her previous ten years cooking professionally and her culinary school education to learn how to make this amazing food.

## Food Carts, Plural

Timber returned to Portland on December 31, 2009, and on April 1, 2010, she opened the Yogio Food Cart specializing in authentic Korean cuisine.

The Red Dragon, home of Timber's Dog House PDX Food Cart.

Yogio received much press and acclaim when it opened; it was even featured on TV. In the fall, Timber got the opportunity to buy another food cart that sold hot dogs at the pod where she was located. She bought that cart, changed the name to the Doghouse and kept going. Timber lovingly refers to that cart as the Red Dragon, unless the transmission goes out—then it is the Red Beast. For a while, Timber ran both food carts.

Timber closed down Yogio on Halloween 2011 because over the time that it was open, she received continuous and ongoing grief for being a "white girl" who was cooking authentic Korean food. Eventually, Timber decided that it was not worth it. Timber actually closed down both carts that day, and she planned to sell one and reopen the other in the spring of 2012. The Yogio cart was sold, and it later became the first Fried Egg I'm in Love food cart.

## A Ten-Year Burger Quest

While growing up in Springdale, Arkansas, Timber loved the burgers they had at the local hamburger joint. That place went out of business while she was in high school, and Timber discovered that no other place in town had patties as good as she was used to. Following college, Timber started cooking professionally, and she began trying to come up with recipes for a seasoning and marinade that matched the burger patties of her childhood.

Over the winter of 2011, Timber finally nailed those recipes, and her ten-year quest was now complete. She was ready to make burgers. When she opened her cart back up on April 1, 2012, it was renamed Timber's Doghouse PDX, and while it still sold incredibly creative tot bowls, the hot dogs were replaced with equally creative hamburgers. Timber's hamburgers are everything that you want in a burger—juicy, tender and perfectly seasoned. I could eat the patty all by itself.

You can get the classics at Timber's, including a cheeseburger and a bacon burger, but you can also get burgers with items like peanut butter, pineapple or roasted garlic truffle aioli. Timber's Doghouse PDX has nothing to do with soccer or hot dogs, but it does have great hamburgers.

*What's Next*: Timber always has something creative and delicious up her sleeve. I am a big fan of hers, and I can't wait to see what is next in her journey.

*When You Go*: Get whichever burger strikes your fancy and make sure to get a tot bowl. Timber's is one of my daughter Zoe's favorite food carts, and Zoe loves the Unexpected Perfection Burger—candied bacon, onions, blue cheese and house three-way mustard. Zoe's favorite tot bowl is the Truffle Treasure Tot Bowl—classic tots topped with chanterelle salt, Asiago cheese and roasted garlic truffle aioli.

# Laissez Les Bon Temps Rouler:
## A Cajun Life

"Have I made a mistake?" That was the question that Chris Fontenot asked himself at the end of the day on July 6, 2012, the first day that his new food cart was open at its Damascus, Oregon location. He had made a *lot* of food, and he had no customers. Not one. Not a singe customer.

Chris's incredible wife, Hillary, told him, "That's ridiculous! They will come." The next day, they did show up, but only three of them. So far, the A

Chris and Hillary Fontenot, owners of the A Cajun Life Food Cart.

Cajun Life Food Cart had been open at its Damascus location for two days, and it was averaging 1.5 customers per day. Let the good times roll!

From those inauspicious beginnings, a great food cart has come into its own. It turned out that Hillary was right. By the fall of 2012, the customers had found out about this food cart on the outskirts of the Portland metro, and they now come in droves from far and wide all the way out to Damascus to get food that is more than worth the drive.

I have worked with scores of small business owners—chefs with big dreams who have started food carts with the hope that they will be able bootstrap their way to a better life. Every week, I tell at least one of these determined entrepreneurs that they need to follow Chris's enterprising example. In my opinion, every food cart owner needs to do what Chris has done, and I am excited to tell you his story.

## Eunice, Louisiana: The Heart of Cajun Country

The A Cajun Life Food Cart specializes in Cajun cuisine. It only has four menu items: Cajun Gumbo, Crawfish Étouffée, Bayou Boogie and Crawfish Pistolettes. Chris is serving the food he grew up eating using family recipes. Chris is from Eunice, Louisiana, the heart of Cajun country.

His gumbo is one of my favorite dishes of all time. I love to bring the white round container that Chris serves his gumbo in up to my lips and take a sip of that deep, rich broth. His gumbo is ethereal. The broth is perfectly seasoned.

Every day that it is open, the food cart has people who used to live in Louisiana and now live in the Northwest make the trek out to Damascus to get themselves some truly authentic Cajun cuisine. Chris has regulars who come from as far away as Salem, Washougal, Beaverton and even Eugene—a two-hour drive.

## Authentic Cajun Cuisine

So what makes the food at A Cajun Life Food Cart truly authentic? A number

of things contribute to the authenticity—the recipes, the seasonings and definitely the ingredients. Chris has his sausage and tasso flown in from Eunice, Louisiana. Chris has a Delta cargo account, and he regularly drives out to Portland International Airport (PDX) to pick up his shipment of Cajun delicacies.

A Cajun Life All-Purpose Cajun Seasoning.

## *Extending the Brand*

One of things that sets A Cajun Life apart from so many other food carts is that in his mind, Chris did not start a food cart—he started a brand, and the food cart was the first step in that brand. In January 2013, Chris asked himself a question that, in my opinion, every food cart owner should ask: "How do we take the next step in developing our brand?"

For Chris and Hillary, the answer was to package and sell A Cajun Life All Purpose Cajun Seasoning. They did a Kickstarter campaign in April to help fund this step, and by July 2013, Chris had 1,100 units of seasoning in his garage ready to sell. There are a number of stores now carrying this awesome seasoning, and that number keeps growing. I encourage every food cart owner to follow in Chris's footsteps. Develop not just a food cart but a brand, and sooner, rather than later, ask yourself how to best extend that brand.

Chris did *not* make a mistake when he started A Cajun Life; in fact, I predict that it will turn out to be one of his best decisions. My food cart hat is off to you, Chris, and as they say in Louisiana, "Laissez les bon temps rouler!"

*What's Next*: Chris has quite a bit planned for A Cajun Life. He is going to add two more flavors to his seasoning line: a Cajun blackening rub and a Cajun chicken rub. He also hopes to add a branded sausage and a branded tasso to his packaged food line. The space that A Cajun Life occupies in Damascus is going to become a four-cart pod, and he is planning to open a second A Cajun Life Food Cart in Portland.

*When You Go*: Get some gumbo and buy a bottle or two of A Cajun Life seasoning.

# Stay Caffeinated, My Friends: Olé Latte Coffee

Todd Edwards opened the Olé Latte Coffee Food Cart in June 2012. The crazy thing is that it was March 2012 when he decided that he was going to open his food cart. He owned a cart by April and began retrofitting, and he was open by June.

## *From Wine Shop to Coffee Cart*

Todd is passionate about wine, and he knows his way around a wine list. Todd is the person you want to have with you at the restaurant when it comes time to pick out a wine to go with your meal. He can look at a wine list and pick a wine that will pair perfectly with your dish. I have seen him use this skill with my own eyes.

For many years, Todd had wanted to open a wine shop. By March 2012, Todd realized that just wasn't going to be in the cards for him to do this. Todd Loves wine, and he also loves coffee. At that time, he did not know coffee like he knew wine. Todd began to educate himself, and he has become quite the coffee aficionado. Today, his food cart is regularly praised in the press as having some of the best coffee in Portland.

## *Time to Name the Cart*

Todd began looking for a name for his coffee cart, and every time he came up with a name he liked, he would see if the domain was available and learn that it was already taken. This happened to Todd repeatedly. Meanwhile, Todd had a running catch phrase that he and his girlfriend, Monica, used. Every time something was great or amazing, as in "that was an amazing breakfast," they would say, "Ole!" One day, it just clicked. He wanted to serve amazing coffee, and the name Olé Latte Coffee was spot on.

## *The Coolest-Looking Espresso Machine You Will Ever See*

As Todd began to educate himself on coffee, he learned that some of the best espresso machines come from La Marzocco, a company that has been making espresso machines since 1927. Todd was able to get his hands on a beautiful red La Marzocco. Ask Todd about his machine when you go to his food cart, and he will passionately tell you why it makes such excellent lattes and espressos.

## The First Year

Todd opened his food cart at a neighborhood food cart pod and hoped for the best. The first year, Todd worked seven days week twelve to sixteen hours a day, and halfway through that first year, they almost closed. Toward the end of 2012, Todd was offered the chance to move to the 10th and Alder food cart pod, and he thought that maybe this location would be the place where they could flourish.

Todd then remembered that his cart serves from the side, and that meant he would need to rent two spaces if he moved to that pod. As fate would have it, two spaces right next to each other were open at 10th and Alder. Todd took both, and the rest is history. His new spot has been wonderful for his business. Downtown turned out to be the perfect place for Todd's cart.

## Burnt Toast

Todd is very proud of the beans they use at Olé Latte, some of which he roasts himself and some he gets from a local Portland roaster, Ristretto Roasters. Todd is very passionate about how long coffee beans should be roasted, and he is not a fan of dark roast coffee. He said that if you toast bread, the flavor improves, but if you burn the toast, you lose the benefit of tasting it. He considers dark roast coffee to be burned.

## Suspended Coffee Comes to Portland

Todd was very grateful for the way that downtown Portland embraced his fledgling business, and he began to look for ways to give back. When he learned about the suspended coffee movement, he immediately put up a suspended coffee board and implemented this wonderful practice, which originally started in Italy, at his cart. The way it works is that if you pay for a suspended coffee, a mark is made on the suspended coffee board indicating that there is a paid-for coffee available for whoever needs it. It is a simple and easy way to give back.

The people who order coffee from the suspended board are people who are homeless or people who are simply down on their luck and not able to currently afford a treat like a latte. For the past year and a half, I have worked extensively with the homeless here in Portland, and doing

Todd Edwards, owner of the Olé Latte Coffee Food Cart.

something like this is much better than giving the homeless cash. Todd has seen people go from being homeless and taking coffee off the suspended board to being gainfully employed and paying for coffee to go onto that board for others in need.

## *The Coffee Truly Is Olé!*

I love the coffee that Todd serves, and his lattes are some of the smoothest and most flavorful I have ever had. Todd has a phrase that he often uses when he ends a social media post: "Stay caffeinated, my friends." I always smile when I see that phrase and think about his amazing coffee.

*What's Next*: Todd's current plans are to open a second cart, also to be located downtown, and then get a third cart that will be mobile and be used for events. Some day, he hopes to open a brick-and-mortar Olé Latte Coffee and own his own roaster.

*When You Go*: Get a latte, and if you like espresso, get a doppio from Todd. I love his doppio. He proudly carries pastries from the Bake Shop Bakery, and you need to buy two of their sweet and salty cookies. They are scrumptious! Get one for now and one to eat when you get home.

*Recipes*: You can find the Olé Latte Coffee recipe for Cold Brew Coffee in *Trailer Food Diaries Cookbook*, Portland edition, vol. 2.

# ABOUT THE AUTHOR

S teven Shomler is a Portland food
writer. He writes about food carts
at Portland Food Cart Adventures,
a website he founded in 2012. As
Steven began writing about food
carts, he fell in love with the people
inside the carts, as well as their
stories. Steven regularly consults with
food cart owners on how to have a
successful startup, coaching them on
topics such as branding, marketing
and social media. Steven is also one
of the founders and organizers of the
Portland Summer Food Cart Festival, which takes place each summer on the
campus of Mt. Hood Community College.

*Photo by Zayne Shomler.*

*Visit us at*
www.historypress.net
......................................................
*This title is also available as an e-book*